press

Jess Ho is best known for their take-no-prisoners opinions on the hospitality industry. They were the food and drink editor for *Time Out Melbourne*, having previously contributed to several bar and restaurant guides for the publication along with countless reviews. Jess has also been published in *The Guardian*, *Foodservice REP*, *Virgin Voyeur*, *Time and Tide* and *Eater* and has contributed to many restaurant guides and cookbooks. Jess is a regular presenter at food and wine events and festivals across Melbourne and has toured large-scale wine events around the country. They've also been a judge on a commercial-network food show, but don't ask them about it unless they've had something very strong to drink. *Raised by Wolves* is Jess's first book.

raised by wolves

Jess Ho

Affirm
press

Published by Affirm Press in 2022
Boon Wurrung Country
28 Thistlethwaite Street,
South Melbourne, VIC 3205
affirmpress.com.au
10 9 8 7 6 5 4 3 2 1

Title: Raised by Wolves / Jess Ho, author
ISBN: 9781922806307 (paperback)

Cover design by: Christa Moffitt
Typeset: J&M Typesetting
Proudly printed in Australia by McPherson's Printing Group

CONTENT NOTE

This work contains discussions of child abuse, sexual harassment, mental illness and suicide.

For Mike

~

If you ask ten people in a room to tell you what happened in the last five seconds, you will receive ten different accounts. This is my non-linear account of the last thirty years. My truth is marred by time, emotion, sleep deprivation, strong opinions and coping mechanisms, but it is my truth. Some names have been obscured, some have been changed, some have not. A few people have been stitched into one for ease of storytelling. If you're in my life and don't recognise yourself in these stories, consider yourself lucky. If you do, I'm sorry.

1

I grew up in restaurants. Not in the way that Asian kids grow up in restaurants because it's the family business, but in the way that dining is a huge part of Chinese culture. Food was the excuse to see each other and connect as a family. Growing up, there were no words of praise, no hugs, no 'I'm so proud' or 'I love you', there was just dinner. Care was expressed by laborious, intricate knife cuts using only a cleaver, simmering a herbal soup to address a minor ailment, slaving over a stove all day to cook my favourite dish, driving several suburbs over to buy a whole fish we couldn't afford and having family banquets.

By the time I started making memories, my family had sold their venue. My dad used to cook with my uncle in a joint venture in Preston back in the eighties. All I know of the place is that it was incredibly hard work with a newborn (I'm referring to my sister; I don't think I was even a smudge in either of my parent's underpants at this stage) and my dad was barely at home, so good riddance to it. The building is still there, functioning as a suburban

Chinese restaurant, but I have never stepped foot inside. I only remember the occasional drive out to Preston where Dad would leave me in the back seat of the car with the window cracked, like a dog, while he picked up cash from being paid out of the business. He'd hand me a bag of warm, greasy prawn crackers to keep me quiet on the drive home. I'd sit with them in my lap, work the knot out with my tiny fingers and split the fried treats with him.

'Don't tell your sister,' he'd say, dreading having to deep fry as soon as he got home.

My childhood revolved around the lazy Susan. I was tucked into a chair against the wall of the local Chinese restaurant, so I couldn't escape, watching my bowl being topped up with herbal soups, crab noodles, steamed fish, clay pot crispy pork, stir fried snow pea shoots, tofu, and eventually, sweet red bean soup followed by cut fruit. I quietly shoveled food into my mouth as I listened to my aunties gossip about their friends I'd never met but would eventually call 'Aunty', watched my cousins complain that their parents didn't order the dish they asked for, heard my mother tell her siblings off for doing stupid shit with their money, while my grandfather sat opposite me, chewing on a fish head, grinning wordlessly like a king presiding over all his spawn, probably thinking to himself, *I made all this*, until the bill arrived and this frail ninety-year-old transformed into a flyweight boxer in a family-wide battle to pay it.

If you haven't seen a five-foot, forty-kilogram man punch your dad (his son) in the head before, you haven't lived. This happened every birthday, promotion, engagement, going away, home-coming, New Year, Chinese New Year, or just because it had been a while.

Booking a table for six somehow always turned into ten. If a cousin couldn't attend, one of the aunties would invite a friend *and* their spouse (and we would be instructed to call them aunty and uncle); if anyone had a visitor over, they might as well come for family dinner. We would manage a way to cram everyone in: we shuffled in or out, shared seats and took turns sitting or standing so everyone would get a chance to eat. Dining made us a community rather than just a family. To this day, if I call someone aunty or uncle, I have to check with my sister to see if we are actually related to them. We never have the answer.

As small children, these dinners always seemed late and long to me and my sister, and we'd be bored before we even got there. Our aunt was known for running on her own time; anyone from my mother's side would be travelling from the other side of the city. My older cousins didn't prioritise family dinners, and by the time they turned up, we always ended up eating way past our bedtime. To keep us occupied, my dad taught us a 'magic trick' where we'd snap toothpicks into the shapes of stars and uncoil them by dropping hot tea into the folds with the end of a chopstick. We were only allowed to do this with our own packet of toothpicks because old Asian men really have a thing for picking food out of their teeth with a stick. We had to make two picks last for the whole dinner. The rest of the time, we just sat there, trying to occupy as little space and airtime as possible until we fell asleep at the table. My dad would carry us into the back seat of the car and buckle us in for the drive home.

Occasionally, strangers would come up to our table and comment on how well behaved my sister and I were, being so young. They'd say that though their own kids were much older than us they still weren't brave enough to bring them for dinner. The reality is, in Asian cultures having children is more than love and lineage. We are a retirement plan, there to serve a purpose. We are raised to fit into our parents' lives; they don't fit around ours. My sister and I were taken to dinners and taught to sit still, eat and listen to what was going on, even if we were too young to understand it. We were taught discipline by being disciplined. If we saw another child throw a tantrum, my sister and I would whisper to each other, 'I wonder if they'll still be alive for the next dinner.'

It was three in the afternoon on a steamy, summer weekday, and I was in a twenty-seater ramen bar hidden in an arcade in the middle of Chinatown in Melbourne's CBD. I was meeting Ronnie, a friend who co-owned a whisky bar. He spent the majority of his pleasure time in Japan, ate like a Tudor royal, worked like a dog and also happened to be Asian, though not the same flavour of Asian as me.

We'd chosen to meet at three because it was before we both had to go to our respective bars to serve drunk people more drinks, it was after the lunch rush so we wouldn't have to wait in line, and we reasoned that the high fat and caloric content of ramen would keep us going until we finished work after one in the morning.

The thing about arcades in Chinatown is there is very little ventilation. I was in a t-shirt, jeans and boots because they were practical and safe to work in, but I could feel myself slowly melting into a puddle while waiting for Ronnie. He arrived wearing pants and a t-shirt, with his long-sleeved work shirt and vest folded under his arm. The lucky bastard had proper air conditioning in his bar because if you kept the room cold, people would keep ordering brown liquor.

The waiter forgoed the usual shout of 'Irasshaimase' as a greeting, and instead, walked over and shook Ronnie's hand. He was so much of a regular that he also had his own secret, off-menu ramen. It was a bowl so rich that you could stand your chopsticks up in it, even before the soup cooled and solidified into a block of flavoured fat, and the noodles were air-dried for twenty-four hours for extra bite. 'Would you like your ramen?' asked the server.

'Two, please.'

'I don't think I could stomach your thick-ass, miso broth and teriyaki chicken concoction on a day like this,' I said, deeply aware that I was gathering underboob sweat when I didn't even have an underboob. I hunched over to prevent the sweat from dripping onto the front of my t-shirt.

'Nah, you'll be fine. We can have it with a beer. They keep their glasses in the freezer.' Ronnie turned his energy to the kitchen and the crew looked up at him, all smiles. 'And two beers, please!'

There were only two staff in the venue – the chef and the waiter – because lunch service was basically over and it had been a slow afternoon. After all, who wants a steaming bowl of ramen when it's so hot you can cook eggs on the pavement? The thing about having Asian blood is that even though my brain had been conditioned to think that it needed cold food on a hot day in Australia, as soon as a bowl of soup was in front of me, I dove into it. What I was really suffering from was a lack of humidity. The dry, Aussie heat didn't just make me eternally thirsty, it also turned me into a husk of a human – irritable and lethargic.

'Irasshaimase!'

I turned my head to the door and saw a pale, sweat-stained family of four who were clearly not from around here. They ignored the *PLEASE WAIT HERE TO BE SEATED* sign and the greeting from the waiter, sat themselves at the only table in the process of being cleaned and grabbed menus off other tables. My first thought whenever I see people act like this is *who raised you?* I looked up at Ronnie and our eyes had a conversation that went something like this:

'They're not from here.'

'Definitely tourists.'

'They're already so rude to the staff.'

'The kids aren't sitting still.'

'This is not going to end well.'

'Look, let's just eat quickly and go.'

The waiter rushed over and tried to explain to the parents how large each bowl of ramen was, how they could customise their bowls with extra toppings and what drinks were on offer, all while wiping down the splashes of broth left behind by the previous diners.

'Can I just get three normal bowls with chicken? The kids will share their bowl.'

'Yes, just to let you know, our standard ramen is pork-based with chashu. Our chicken ramen is a little spicy.'

'Just make the chicken not spicy.'

'The chicken is marinated with spice already.'

'Fine, just the normal ramen. And some forks.'

'Yes, of course.'

I took in long, slow breaths and told myself not to work up a rage-induced fever before having to run around in circles in a bar all evening. Ronnie and I spoke about the usual things we spoke about: if we ate anywhere good recently, how busy the nights had been, how our mutual friends were, if we had tasted any decent products recently, where we wanted to go on holiday (or in Ronnie's case, when he would next go back to Japan), how tired we were, if there were any new late-night venues to eat at that wouldn't put us in a food coma after work, but eventually, possibly inevitably, we landed on the topic of poorly behaved guests.

'Some genius thought he was being inconspicuous by going to the bathroom every five minutes, not eating any food, ordering the most expensive wine on the list and harassing women from the other tables to join him. When I went to check the state of the bathrooms, I saw that he left his bag of coke on the cistern. Then he tried to come behind the bar and play bartender, which made me snap. How the fuck do people not know the difference between their space and our space?' I said.

'What did you do?'

'Made him pay his bill and didn't even mention his bag. He was either so completely blasted he didn't notice that he left it behind, or he had a shitload more on himself.'

'It's not that bad where we are. We just get hens parties on their way from one venue to another. They kill time at the bar and leave it in a mess. They're harmless,' said Ronnie. A small bowl rolled under our table with a trail of noodles and broth leading to the family. The kids were having a mini food fight while the parents ate in silence. I glanced at the waiter, who was standing at the bar with an awkward smile, watching the mess radiate out to the whole dining room.

There is no right thing to do in this situation. As a front-of-house person, if you ask the table to control their kids, they yell at you and say that you're discriminating against them and ruining their dining experience. If you tell the children to go back to their seats and ask them to stop throwing food, the parents will yell at you and tell you not to parent their kids. If you go over and start cleaning up around them, the parents will treat you like a free cleaner and babysitter while they let chaos unfold. If you ask them to leave, you forfeit the bill and you're left with a mess you were going to clean up anyway. The waiter was probably taking the most passive and smart approach to the situation, even if it wasn't the easiest one. I saw this situation as an omen and began to dread the nine hours ahead of me.

One of the kids started screaming like they were auditioning for a slasher flick and throwing noodles against the wall. Ronnie and I rolled our eyes at each other.

We both worked in bars because we thought we would be protected from the mess that is diners with children, but we were wrong. The liquor licence both our venues had been granted didn't allow anyone under the age of eighteen to enter the bar. We assumed there would be no confusion about children dining while parents drank because neither of us worked in a pub and drinks were clearly both venues' focus. Regardless, I still had people bring in their children, allowing them to crawl all over the floor after a Friday night service when multiple glasses would shatter without failure and no amount of sweeping could ensure we recovered every single speck. I informed parents of fines and what it would mean for us to have a red mark against the venue with the Victorian Commission for Gambling and Liquor Regulation. I explained the law, the rights as the licensee and the dangerous combination of broken glass and filthy bar floor, but people didn't care. Or at least, they didn't care until the second something went wrong. Then it was everyone's fault but their own. Luckily in a ramen bar, the only really bad thing that could happen to a child was a chopstick in the eye. It was a small comfort that this family asked for forks.

'Can you imagine if we behaved like that if we were kids?' said Ronnie.

'I wouldn't be alive. If I survived, I'd probably be walking with a limp.'

Ronnie and I might have had different cultural upbringings, but we feared the same things. Asian parents are known for being resourceful and ruthless. All the ones I know collect and reuse plastic bags and containers until they shred or become rigid and shatter from over-washing. They can save seeds from any fruit or vegetable and miraculously grow an entire crop from it. But most importantly, they can turn anything into a weapon.

Every time I walked past a pair of those two-dollar slippers you can buy in Chinese grocers, I thought about my mother taking it off her foot and smashing me on the back of the head with it for being late to the dinner table, even though I was late because I was finishing the endless tutoring homework my parents made me do so I could get a scholarship into one of the handful of Ho family–approved private schools. When I saw those slippers lined up near the entrance of a house, I would rub my skull. I could feel how hard and rigid the plastic slippers were just by looking at them. Bamboo canes were used to whip my back so I would sit up straight and not hunch. There were times I would be practising piano and I'd feel a searing pain across my kidneys for leaning over the keys rather than sitting up straight. Rulers and protractors were rapped across my fingers for playing wrong notes even though I was sightreading classical songs I had never heard before. My sister and I were convinced that my mother had a huge crush on our piano teacher, and she wanted us to be prodigies so it would reflect well on her. I became a victim of coathanger attacks every time she came to pick me up from my hour lesson and our teacher would say, 'She has the talent, but not the passion. Her sister has the passion, but not the talent.' My mother took it personally that together we were her perfect child, but individually we were just disappointments.

As I grew older and spoke with other Asian kids, we normalised our unconventional punishments and laughed about how no time out or grounding would ever produce the high-achieving workhorses we were during school. It may have been viewed as abusive, but we would never disrespect our elders. It was ingrained in our culture. When we heard how often our friends would scream at their parents to fuck off, we'd sit there with our mouths open and wonder if they would have a home to go back to. At a certain stage, my sister told me to stop talking to people about how I was disciplined. It wasn't normal, she said. She didn't want me to get into any more trouble. I didn't know what she meant at the time.

As we paid for our meals at the counter, Ronnie leaned in close and whispered to me, 'You know what these children need?'

'Asian parents,' I replied, and we chuckled quietly with the wait staff.

2

Every decent hospitality worker I know has worked at one of the Big Four. In hospitality, the Big Four aren't the Commonwealth Bank, ANZ, Westpac and NAB, they're McDonald's, Hungry Jack's, KFC and Pizza Hut. It doesn't matter how many hatted restaurants you've worked at, how many wine shows you've judged or scholarships you've won, you make sure to leave your training at one of the Big Four on your resume. To any manager, it's proof that you can adhere to company policy and procedure. You've been drilled, prodded and tested by international consistency standards. You have been taught to multitask. You are not intimidated by a docket machine endlessly spitting out tickets. You've worn the most demeaning and recognisable uniforms and kept yourself clean and presentable. You've seen people at their worst and served them with a smile. You have worked for the most minimal wages.

In short: you are easy to mould.

My first job was at [redacted].

The week before I turned fourteen and nine months, I dropped my resume to every shitty retail and hospitality venue looking for part-time staff in the city. I secretly wanted to work at JB Hi-Fi, but [redacted] called me first. I was desperate for a taste of independence, some responsibility and a reason not to go home. If I was making a few dollars doing it, even better. I didn't have any friends, so it wasn't like I could bum around the city after school, looking for trouble.

When I turned up to induction, there was one other person. She was a few years older than me, had plasters over the tops of her ears, nose and eyebrow to cover her piercings and wore a bold lip liner that was ten shades darker than her skin tone. This wasn't her first part-time job, and she was already bored by the whole process. I was nervous as hell.

Our boss was straight out of a comedy sketch set in a crappy fast-food franchise. She looked like she had lived in the back office for the last decade; was more over it than the hormonal, overly pierced inductee who wouldn't make it past induction; and relished in telling her staff everything they were doing wrong, rather than showing them how to do it right. The front of house staff disliked her. The back of house staff despised her. I had no opinions on her until she told me our uniforms would be deducted from our first pay, and we would be charged for all the post mix we consumed. Meanwhile, she often ordered the kitchen crew to make her dinner. It took me two shifts to pay off my hideous, oversized uniform. 'Don't worry,' she told me, 'It's a bond. When you finish up with the company and return your uniform, you get the money back.'

I was being paid five dollars and twenty-six cents per hour because it was one cent more than minimum wage. Gotta start somewhere, I told myself.

To call what we were serving 'food' would be a generous generalisation. There wasn't a single bit of produce that arrived at the restaurant in its raw, recognisable form. Everything came in a box with formulas written on the side. Cheese was tubular or already shredded and sealed in bags as large as my torso. Toppings arrived in jars or cans, or pre-sliced in bags. The soft serve came as a powder and had to be inspected for cockroaches or rat faeces before it was blended with water and dropped into the machine. Everything past what the customers could see smelled like rot smothered in rancid grease.

It was a good shift if I didn't find insects in my bag when I changed to go home, because the venue was on the second floor of an old building owned by cheap landlords. I lasted six months. Barely. I counted down the days, only so I could add it to my resume. The store was shut down less than a year later.

Part-time jobs came easily after I had the smallest bit of experience down on my CV. I scored jobs doing data entry, in a call centre, as a video store clerk, in retail and in cafes until I fell into a job that wasn't just turning up and then getting paid.

I'd just turned eighteen and was in my first semester of a very cruisy creative arts degree when I was hired as a waiter at a fancy inner-city pub. I'd been smart enough to get my Responsible Service of Alcohol certificate before I was old enough to serve alcohol, and had received all my qualifications for back-of-house at high school thanks to some optional units they were offering at the time. But this was a front-of-house role. As with most situations where someone who is wildly unqualified is hired in a decent venue, they were desperate for staff and I happened to be there at the right time. It was the first job I was tipped at (good tips, too), and it was the job where I received my first taste of wine education. I had to learn the menu inside and out, and I worked with chefs who made everything from scratch.

It was the first time I had colleagues who took pride in their work. The head chef was David, a neurotic South African with wild eyes who darted around constantly to make sure everything was up to his exacting standards. His mild-mannered sous never said two words during service but could make the most cutting observation of the night over knock-off drinks, and the commis (the most junior chef in the kitchen) was a good-value bogan whose superpower was getting the job done well and fast. Then there was our dishie. Even though the rest of the kitchen staff were higher ranked than he was, they worshipped him. He was a Chinese exchange student studying something to do with computer engineering. He helped to prep food without complaint and did some of the restaurant's graphic design work for free. He was the smartest person in any room he walked into, but he'd never let you know it. He also let the kitchen staff call him Gary because none of them could pronounce his real name, and they thought they'd assimilate him with the friendliest bogan name possible. If I saw him on the street today, I would still call him Gary.

The owners were a couple who bought the gastropub off well-seasoned publicans. Their first move was their smartest: they retained all their core staff and didn't promote themselves above anyone. The holiday season was coming up and all the casual staff moved on, because that's just what happens. It's the hospitality version of 'new year, new me,' only everything is the same and you're just carrying different food in a different setting. While I was hired by one of the owners, I was trained by the venue manager. Jodi was a Kiwi in her mid-twenties, the first in a long line of Kiwis I would work with in hospitality. She set the tone for all Kiwis that succeeded her: fun-loving hard workers who could drink their body weight in alcohol every night. She taught me how to properly present myself to tables, memorise specials, open wine in front of guests, check for faults, run a function, and to deal with entitled people and still get tipped. She also taught me how to drink until the early hours of the morning and sort myself out so I could still work a double the next day.

The other crew who worked the floor included a tall, tanned and handsome rich kid, who was trying to prove to himself that he didn't need his parents' money, and Sandra, who had worked as a waitress the whole time she'd been at uni. Even though Sandra was part time, she cared about the business and genuinely wanted everyone to enjoy themselves. The local rambling drunks who came in to sink pints and chat someone's ear off loved her. The bar work was split between one of the owners and Andy, a country kid who was the bar manager, and who would always refer to *the* bar as '*my* bar' to purposely drive the owner insane.

This would be the best team I'd ever work with.

'I'm suffering,' said Jodi. 'Do you wanna split a minge?'

'A what?' I was scrounging around in the waiters' station looking for a notepad and pen before we started service.

'Jodi calls bottles of sparkling mineral water "minges",' said one of the waiters, clocking in for his shift.

Jodi cracked a bottle before we even responded, divided it between three glasses and hid them next to the POS system in the station.

'What did you do last night?' I asked.

'Andy and I went to Gerald's 'cause he'd never been. For some reason I let him pick every bottle and he kept choosing big reds,' she said.

'It was thirty degrees last night.'

'That's why I need a minge.'

Jodi briefed me and the other waiter next to the basket of

sourdough that the kitchen made for every service. She lobbed off a butt piece, took a cold pat of butter out of its foil, stacked it on like a piece of cheese and bit into it, leaving distinct teeth marks in the fat.

'I'm gonna need you two to help me out in the dining room tonight,' she said. 'It's not crazy, but if you could check in on me occasionally to make sure everything is stocked and to help run food and clear, that would be great.'

The venue was made up of three sections: the bar, the bistro and the dining room, each with a different menu and style of service. The bar's food and service was the most casual, and the dining room was the most fussy, which meant our regulars were anything from students to CEOs who lived in the area. The bistro was somewhere in between and the busiest section of the pub most nights of the week. We always rotated which waiters worked which section so we wouldn't get bored and tips would even out, but the kitchen served all three sections at once. This meant they were pumping out perfectly rare-cooked venison pithiviers in a house-made puff pastry with pickled wild mushrooms on a celeriac puree, next to endless orders of chips and gravy. David, the head chef, didn't like to make things easy on himself, and even though he was scooping out litres of gravy into little boats for the bar every night, he insisted on making it from the fond and drippings collected from prepping dishes in the dining room. This meant that everyone in the bar would be eating the best chips and gravy they'd ever had, and David would have to scrape up more and more orders while trying to concentrate on his more intellectual dishes, which would make him explode with fury. His rage was always illogical and hilarious, and I often caught him yelling at lemon halves that he'd accidentally squirted into his own eye.

'Tell me this, Jessie.' David was the only person in the world whom I would ever let call me Jessie, mainly because I was too afraid to correct him. 'Why don't these people order real food if the gravy is so good? People should trust me to cook more than gravy. Isn't it your job to make them order a plate of food? Why don't you do it, yeah?'

As the last hire, I couldn't tell him what he already knew – that people were cheap and he was making the chips and gravy too delicious for the bar flies to want to order anything else.

'Oh yeah, what do you want me to sell?'

'The sausages. I make a different batch every time we run out and these are beautiful, yeah. It's pub food, yeah?'

'What's the count on sausages?'

'I have twelve serves.'

'If I sell them all, can I come in and learn how to make them from you?'

'You sell them first, yeah?'

I had two hours until the kitchen closed, but the bar and bistro were already clearing out. It wasn't a busy night and the kitchen called it at nine. By the end of service, I'd sold eleven plates.

'Nice try, Jessie. I'll let you keep your job.' David put a plate of sausages on the pass.

'I've already taken out all the food for the front,' I said.

'That plate is for you guys. You have to taste it, so you know what you're selling next time. Come in tomorrow at eight in the morning and I'll show you how to make them.'

'Really?' I asked. The kitchen crew looked at me through the pass in disbelief while they packed away their sections.

'If you keep asking me, I might change my mind.'

The commis chef cracked a smile. This was the David he knew.

'A pint each for the kitchen, please,' David added. 'We will be out in about twenty.'

By the time we all knocked off, the kitchen crew were still sitting at the bar in their leather pants and jackets, each resting one arm on their helmets. They hardly ever stuck around because they all rode motorcycles to and from work, but this was a special occasion.

'I'm cleaning the lines,' said Andy, using his chin to point out the endless jugs of beer on the bar, 'Come help us out.'

I grabbed a pot glass and sat down next to the sous chef. 'What's this one?'

'Free,' he said, and took a sip. 'I heard you're coming in tomorrow to make sausages with David.'

'Yeah. I'm keen!'

'Why would anyone be keen to spend time with David when

they don't have to?' he said, and laughed to himself. 'Be careful, he might try to recruit you to the kitchen.'

I heard a tapping on the window and turned around. It was Jodi's and Sandra's boyfriends. I unlocked the side door and let them in.

'Do you wanna tell our girlfriends to pick up their phones?'

'I think they're getting changed. Here for the beers?'

'Always.'

Jodi's and Sandra's boyfriends worked in the best and second-best restaurants in Melbourne, respectively. No one ever said anything when we were sitting around the bar drinking free beer, but we all knew that, professionally and socially, we were punching above our weight. When we debriefed on our nights, we'd laugh about who won the bet over whether the 'Mercedes' function was for the car dealership up the road or a twenty-first birthday party for a cashed-up bogan's daughter. The fact that it was a fifty-fifty chance said a lot about where we worked. When the boyfriends joined us, they would tell stories about how some rich guy had asked for a three-hundred-dollar steak to be cooked well done and then complained that it was taking too long, or how an international celebrity came in, drank a terrible vintage wine from a good producer, ordered half the menu and would only push food around their plate. On numerous occasions, they were instructed to never look directly at the celebrity.

The boyfriends would also take out wads of cash from their

pockets, peel off a couple of twenties and leave it for the drinks they consumed while we had our knock-offs. They rationalised that someone had to pay for the beer, and it might as well be them, otherwise the owners would think they were stealing from them. It turns out that the cash wasn't their pay, but their weekly tips, which was enough for them to live off. Those were the good old days of corporate entertainment budgets and company credit cards being used for tips. I could see how some people made a career out of hospitality; all it took was getting a job in the right place before the Global Financial Crisis. 'I can't drink any more beer,' I said, pushing away my glass.

'It might be free, but it tastes like shit,' said Sandra.

'That's why I'm cleaning the lines,' said Andy, gesturing to the taps while hunched over in the bar, annoyed at us for stating the obvious.

'How long do you have left?' said Jodi.

'Well, I have to clean your glasses and jugs, drain the dishwasher and run the chemical through. Not long.' Andy couldn't wait for us to leave.

'Then you won't mind if we go get some drinks down the road instead of hanging around? Are you cool to lock up?' Jodi was already halfway out the door.

'Tony's or cocktails?'

'Whichever is open. We'll text you,' Jodi yelled from the street.

***

We called the bar 'Tony's' because it was owned by one of our regulars named Tony. None of us knew what his bar was called, even though we were there every second night. When he wasn't working at his venue, he'd be drinking at ours. We'd fling him a free drink or a snack, and he always took care of us in return. Tony's was a late-night sports bar that was aggressively lit, didn't serve top-shelf spirits, only had beer out of cans and got around the food service clause in liquor licensing by serving beer nuts and packet crisps. And it closed at 3am. We loved it there.

Jodi came back to the table with a tray of gin and tonics and started rolling a cigarette.

'I'm finally feeling better,' said Jodi.

'Yeah,' I said, 'when it's time to go to bed.'

Tony came out and put down a paper plate stacked with party pies and sausage rolls. He dug around in his apron and rained down tabs of tomato sauce.

'I was just making myself a snack. I thought you might be hungry. I got a toaster oven and a pie warmer from a garage sale. Best things I ever bought for the office.'

'Yes! Sausage rolls,' said Andy. 'Tony, you're the best.' He sat down and started drinking the closest gin and tonic to him.

'So why all the red wine last night, Andy? You almost killed Jodi,' said David.

'Hang on, hang on. I didn't almost kill her. And she let me pick the wine.'

'You didn't have to pick such high-alcohol heavy reds for a summer night,' said Jodi as she took the lid off a party pie and filled the insides with sauce.

'You didn't say anything! I like what I like.'

'How did you get home? I was in the gutter waving down taxis until one of them finally picked me up.' Jodi was always a class act.

'I slept in my car. Actually, that's a lie. I was so drunk I couldn't get my key in the lock. I slept *next to* my car and woke up when someone walked their dog this morning and checked that I was alive.'

'Andy!' David was not impressed. He grew up rough so he was always on high alert and looking over his shoulder. I loved hearing about everyone's antics because I had never been that free in my life. I was relatively new to drinking and only sank pints to blow off steam for an hour or so after work.

'I'm fine,' Andy said. 'I did it all the time back home.'

'Yeah, but you're not back home. You're in Melbourne. You can't do shit like that, yeah?' Occasionally, David got all paternal on us. Not just because he was the oldest of us all, but because he was practising for when he would be a father in six months. 'Anyways, guys. I'm off. See you at 8am, Jessie. Don't be late or I won't like you anymore.'

'Yeah, yeah, see you at eight.'

At 7.55am, I knocked on the back door that led to the kitchen. There was no answer. I waited a few minutes and knocked again.

Gary opened the door for me, hands wet from whatever work he was doing.

'David's trying to make himself a coffee. Do you want to help him?'

'I can't make coffee either.'

'Good luck,' he said, and went back to scrubbing potatoes.

'Fuck! Damn it!' I heard the unmistakeable sound of coffee beans bouncing on tiles. Once I walked out of the kitchen and into the bar, I could see that David had tried to pour beans into the grinder while the lid was still on. 'Jessie, your first job is to make me a coffee.'

I didn't even know how to turn the coffee machine on, let alone operate it. The trays were all drying in a rack along with the group heads and baskets, and the puzzle of assembling it intimidated the hell out of me. 'I can't make coffee. Andy does them all. I can go out and buy you a coffee and not break the only machine in the building, though.'

David reached above him and switched on the kettle. 'Tea. We are all drinking tea. Jessie, sweep up the beans, yeah?'

When I came back into the kitchen, David was cutting up a pig that was on its back, belly open and hollowed out, exposing its ribs from the inside. He was biting the edge of his lip and concentrating so hard that Gary stopped working, raised his index finger to his mouth and shook his head. I could imagine David throwing a tantrum at the pig's corpse because the butchery had gone wrong or he had accidentally nicked himself. Not this time, though. David separated the shoulders of the pig with a few swift movements, and Gary exhaled, turned around and went back to work.

'Look here, Jessie. The pork is very cold. Touch it.' David grabbed my hand and placed it on the pig. 'Straight out of the fridge because you don't want to turn it into a paste. I'm going to cut up the meat and chill it again. The grinder is in the freezer, yeah.'

'Okay, wow.'

'If any part of this process is done warm, it's not going to taste right. You'd have to start over. It's why I do it early, before I turn on any of the equipment. It's going to be a push to get the bread in the oven for lunch, but we don't have any bookings for the dining room until one, anyway.'

David started throwing chunks of meat into a large plastic container and observed the weight. He was so lost in his task that he completely forgot I was in the room and started pouring spices into the mix and massaging it through without saying anything. He clicked the lid on top, opened the freezer, threw it in, turned around and saw me standing there, waiting as still and as silent as I could be.

'I told my wife that one of the waiters wanted to learn how to make sausages. I was really suspicious of you, but she told me that it was a good thing that you wanted to know. She's a better judge of people than I am.'

'Clearly she hasn't met me.'

'That's what I told her, Jessie. If you're wondering what I just did, I seasoned the mixture and it's going in the freezer before it's ground because I handled it and warmed it up with my body temperature. I like to use natural casing, so we're going to put that in warm water. Do you know what casing is made of?'

'Intestine.'

'Good, Jessie.' I wondered if he was going to talk to his child like this. Over the next couple of hours, David would go back and forth from chilling meat to processing it, and eventually packing it into its casing, making imperceptible movements to create links and chains. It was the first time I'd seen David glide through his work. Up until this point, I'd only seen him freak out at inanimate objects and force his body into shapes that looked uncomfortable for him to hold, and were uncomfortable for us to look at. After completing the chain of sausages, he held the links up with a hook and smiled – another first. I'd seen him pump out hundreds of convoluted plates of food at this point, but this was the first time he looked pleased with his work.

'We're going to hang these in the cool room for at least twenty-four hours.'

'Why's that?'

'A few reasons. The flavours will settle and develop in the meat, the mixture binds together properly so it is the texture of sausage, and it just cooks better that way. The skins won't burst because they've had time to dry.'

'So, I take it we don't have sausages on for today.'

'Yes, Jessie. Good work. Are you on for lunch? Do you have to go?'

'I've got class but I'm working tonight.'

'See you for dinner. Go and learn things so you don't have to be a chef when you grow up, yeah.' I knew he was joking, but he also wasn't.

When I came back for dinner, the kitchen crew were uncharacteristically warm towards me. I'd gone from the green-as-fuck new chick who might only last a few months, to someone David wanted to keep around. They all made a point to say hi to me when I dumped my bag in the back, and they didn't boss me around for pitchers of iced water as I was getting changed.

'What did you do to David this morning?' asked Jodi. 'He's never nice to people. You know, like, he's nice, but he's not *nice*.'

'Nothing. I barely even said anything. I didn't even help him. I just watched.'

'Well, he told me he likes you 'cause you're not dumb. Usually he asks me when I'm getting a new waiter and then lists off all the things they've done wrong in a single service.'

'Better than pissing him off.'

Service was a breeze because for the first time in a week none of the staff were hungover, diners were in a rush to get out and most of the patrons were more interested in drinking in the front bar with bags of crisps. It was too hot for hot chips and gravy. Jodi and I cleaned down all the tables, reclothed the dining room and set for the next day's lunch bookings, then the kitchen rang the bell for service.

'It's beer time,' said Jodi.

'Hey, get Jessie here,' said David, 'I want to ask her a question. You stick around, too.' Jodi motioned for me to gather in. I made my way to the pass.

'We've got a table tomorrow. Eight people. Mum's birthday. No share food. They want classic European food because that's what Mum likes. We've sorted out the entree and main. What do you think for dessert?'

'What kind of European food are you cooking?'

'French-ish. Ambient seafood to start. Duck for mains. We'll do some classic sides. Get Gaz to turn some veg.'

'How old's Mum?'

'Seventy.'

When I did my placements for my back-of-house certificates, I was assigned to a private women's club where the youngest member was sixty-five. We had profiles on every single person so we knew what diet they were on, what they were allergic to, and what their doctors told them to avoid eating. All of them preferred their food on the softer side, and I once had a fruit plate sent back to the kitchen because 'the grapes were too much hard work'.

'Look, I don't want to sound like a know-it-all teenager, even though that's what I am, but I find after a certain age, people don't enjoy chewing too much or trying new things. You're gonna be cooking for other tables and you want something easy to turn out. Just do a perfect crème caramel. And then they won't carry on about it being too heavy or ruining their diet and all those other things people say when dessert comes out.'

The sous chef looked at David and said, 'That works for me.'

'Yeah, not a bad idea, Jessie.'

'How's the recipe box?'

'No crème caramel.'

'Girlfriends?'

'Girlfriends.'

'Oh, you're gonna love this,' said Jodi.

I watched the kitchen crew scurry towards the nook near where they kept their bags. They retrieved two books. One was Stephanie Alexander's *The Cook's Companion* and the other was Maggie Beer's *Harvest*. David took one book and sat on the bench with his dirty kitchen clogs dancing on the ends of his toes. Sous Chef sat on the counter on the opposite side of the room. They both looked up at each other, grinned and cracked the already tattered spines of their respective books.

'Give me eggs,' David yelled.

'Two whole, two yolk.'

'I have four whole. Okay, now sugar.'

'Two tablespoons in the egg mixture, a cup for the caramel.'

'Mine are all in grams. I have a split of milk and cream. You?'

'No cream. Just milk.'

'I think I've just won.'

'I do, too.' Sous Chef closed his book, resting it on his lap, and David looked at his cover.

'Maggie wins again.' David jumped off the counter and towards the whiteboard covered in prep and ordering notes. In the top corner were an 'M' and an 'S', each with a tally beside it. I'd always wondered what it stood for but never had the balls to ask. Over my employment at the pub, I learned the richer recipe would always win. Measurements in grams would also earn you points. A way to repurpose ingredients like egg yolks or whites also scored you an easy win. Maggie had two extra points on the score board. I'd never met Stephanie, but she seemed like a hardworking and competitive woman. She wouldn't be happy about this.

Jodi and I went back to the dining room, polishing buckets of cutlery and counting off what we needed for lunch service.

'David has never asked a front-of-house person for their opinion before. This is going to make everyone's lives easier.'

''Cause he won't be trying to push me out?'

'It's been a while since he warmed to a new front-of-house person.'

'When was the last time?'

'Sandra.'

'She's worked here for years!'

'Exactly. Now I can stop worrying about constantly hiring staff. He usually breaks them.'

'He's harmless. Not even abusive.' I thought about all the times I had been spoken to like a servant by a customer. Then I thought about the time my mother threw a dishrack full of wet plates, knives and pots at me from across the room when she said I drank my cup of tea too loudly. I was five. 'He's not abusive at all.'

There wasn't much of a divide between the front and back of house, but after my introduction to sausages, any suggestion of a wall had collapsed. The kitchen crew were more than happy to show me how to make sourdough, shuck oysters, walk me through the simple butchery of the whole four-legged animals we served in the restaurant, and would enthusiastically ask me to taste new dishes before they made it onto the menu. In return, I took them to dine in restaurants that weren't written about in food magazines and explained Chinese cooking techniques and how the textures we desired seemed like an aggressive sensory assault to the Western palate. We'd pool all our tips to buy a bottle of wine none of us could afford, or save to eat at a restaurant we would probably never be skilled enough to work at, and were too poor to experience twice. When I dined without the kitchen crew, I'd steal copies of menus as souvenirs and pore over them with the chefs. They'd drill me on what I ate, what was on the plate and how everything was cooked while they reverse-engineered the cost of the dish in their heads and called bullshit on the whole experience. If I fell for any gimmicks, they'd laugh at me and explain that I'd just got played. This was the mid-2000s – a time when restaurants didn't have Twitter accounts, phones didn't have cameras, Instagram didn't exist, food television hadn't exploded and everyone competitively chased hats. The world seemed larger, there was less exposure, zero romanticism and more at stake. I fucking loved it.

Though I'd started my degree with plans to become a writer, hospitality wasn't looking like such a bad way to earn a living, at least for now. My part-time pub hours were already more than my full-time university contact hours – eighteen hours a week of overthinking, movie-watching and reading that would eventually earn me a degree in pretentiousness. My job wasn't respectable (every time I told someone I was a waiter, they'd speak to me like I was dumb), but I was proud of the team I worked with, the food on the plate and the experience we delivered. When we drank at the end of every shift, it was to celebrate the service, not commiserate our life choices. We were each other's counsel over relationship breakdowns, regrets and crises. We were present at births, graduations, marriages and funerals. Eventually, we all moved on to new venues or careers, and we kept in touch until life got in the way. Years after we'd all left, the owners sold up and pursued their new dream of small-scale, independent beer production.

For a brief moment, I'd felt like I actually mattered to a small group of people, and that we could depend on each other. I didn't know it at the time, but I'd be chasing this feeling for the rest of my career.

3

It's an understatement to say that I was a very particular child. Everything had to be just so or I'd be in a state of discomfort. I was always anxious. Anxious that I was going to be yelled at by my dad. Anxious that I was going to get the shit kicked out of me by my mother. Anxious that my very flimsy grasp of the English language was going to reveal how Chinese I was to my low-socioeconomic, underfunded, poorly educated, racist breeding ground of a primary school. Anxious that these poorly educated and ignorantly racist kids would follow me and beat me up on the way home from a day of being told to smile while learning the alphabet. Anxious that my tiny hands didn't have the dexterity to play Mozart while I sat on a phone book on top of an adjustable piano stool. Anxious that I would develop high blood pressure and would have to take a tablet every day like my dad. Anxious that the harsh Australian sun would give me cancer and I'd have chunks of my face carved out and displayed during Show and Tell, like the parents who came to warn us about UV rays. Anxious that I would get sick. Anxious that I dressed funny. Anxious that I had no friends. Anxious that the teachers could see that I had no friends, and everyone could sense how much pity they had for me. Anxious that everyone could see that we were poorer than everyone else. Anxious that people knew I was eating food that was seen as scraps by butchers, fishmongers and green grocers. Anxious that I was allergic to everything. Anxious that I was going to have another asthma attack. Anxious that our house would burn down in my sleep. Anxious about falling asleep. Anxious that I couldn't control absolutely everything that was happening all the time. Before I even really understood the concept of death, I was anxious of dying and being conscious of a perpetual nothingness. I was that dumbass child who wished they were a tree because they were the oldest things on the planet and my undeveloped brain wanted the longest possible life. I'd read about an immortal jellyfish once, but I don't like water, so that was that.

As a kid, I reasoned the opposite of death is cleanliness. If you're clean, you can't get sick, and if you're not sick, you can't die. The first time we found a mouse in the house, I thought I was going to contract the bubonic plague – despite being vaccinated and having access to modern medicine. Ring Around the Rosie made a very strong impression on me. It didn't make sense to me that we would all skip around in a circle asking for tissues and flowers and pass out for fun. So, being the naturally nosy person I was (encouraging teachers would call me curious, but we all know primary school teachers are a soft touch), I spent my time after school in the local library researching the origins of this nonsensical nursery rhyme until I worked myself up into a paranoid, hygiene-obsessed loop.

We also kept chickens. Not the cute, fluffy kind that you see at the markets or children's farms, but the large, aggressive layer hens that were the same size as me as a toddler, flapping their shit-stained wings all over the place while trampling their own faeces, pecking at grain that had been rolling around in their excrement and screeching incessantly like people who always want to talk to the manager. And we had a rooster that lived up to every stereotype that Warner Brothers cartoons would attribute to it. It was loud, it was filthy and it was an arsehole. My dad built a pen for the birds, but once a day, he would let them out to roam all over our backyard, shit all over the joint and chase me around until I'd hide inside the house with my asthma puffer, convinced they had flapped some kind of virus all over me that would enter my bloodstream and take control of all of my facilities.

It wasn't until my dad decided to bond with me by making dinner together, that I eventually started being less anxious about everything. He could sense that I was afraid of the entire world and he wanted to change that. The first time we cooked together, he grabbed a few bricks, a bowl, a bucket filled with boiling water and his cleaver. He walked into the backyard and let the chickens out to terrorise me. He chased one around the garden for a few minutes and brought it over by the neck. In my mind, its talons grew to twice their size and it was scratching around the air while flapping for freedom, convinced it could somehow fly out of my dad's grasp. His laugh at its powerlessness didn't unsettle me or make me think that he was a serial killer in the making. It comforted me, because for the first time since we got the chickens, I thought to myself, *You stupid bird.*

Then, my dad did something completely irresponsible but completely in line with his parenting style. He handed his cleaver over to me as he held down the neck of this bird and said, 'You do it.' There was no question as to what I was going to do. One of my strongest memories as a child is of my dad laying out Chinese newspaper on the tiles of the kitchen once a week, securing his chopping board and smashing through the bones of a whole steamed chicken with the proficiency of the men at the Chinese barbecue chop shop. I knew I wasn't going to tickle this bird to death with the blunt end of a cleaver, which had travelled all the way to Taylors Lakes from Dad's destitute village in Hong Kong.

I was a very weedy kid and swinging this cleaver took the force of my entire body. Naturally, I did not kill the chicken in one stroke. It took a few chops, accompanied by my dad laughing at how difficult it was for me to kill something that was pinned down like Catherine of Aragon making way for the Reformation. Well, another kind of reformation was happening, because when the head of the chicken finally rolled off the stack of bricks and I watched my dad drain the blood into a bowl to be steamed into jelly for congee, pluck its feathers and remove its guts, I felt some kind of confidence for the first time in my life. Sure, I had killed a living thing, but the infectious disease that my mind inoculated it with did not exist, and I watched it literally being stripped down to become nothing more than food. This is probably how King Henry VIII felt when he established the Church of England. It's way too much power for a seven-year-old to handle. Just like the Catholic church, my father created a monster.

I slowly got over all the things that made me anxious. Dirt? Let me roll in it. The cold? I'll run around in a singlet for the whole afternoon. Being identified as Chinese? Yeah! Just look at my face. Friends? Don't need them! Not excelling at piano? My piano teacher can suck it! Bullying? I've killed a chicken; I can kill you too! Not finishing homework? Are you kidding, I finished it in class while completely ignoring the authority of my teachers. Death? I had no idea what it was like before I was born, and I'll have no idea when I'm gone.

I thought I had gotten rid of all my anxieties until I started working in bars and restaurants. I thought I knew what to expect. In my mind, men's toilets would be the worst: flooded with urine, filled with other bodily fluids, stained with shame, barely sanitised, lacking toilet paper, blocked with shit-stained clothing, filled with flies, a breeding ground for maggots, lacking ventilation, shielded from the cleansing sun, festering and baking in its own grime.

Depending on the venue, maybe add a glory hole.

I was wrong.

Women's toilets are much worse.

After leaving the fancy pub I mostly ignored my creative arts degree and instead focused on a series of front-of-house roles, plus a brief stint in restaurant PR. After Twitter exploded and I became known online for my sassy takes on 2011 dining culture, I accepted a role to launch a new restaurant. 'Authentically Thai' was how it was pitched to me, but I saw no Thai people in the executive team. I was orginally brought on to manage the social media presence, launch the venue digitally and work as a host, but it became a lot more than that. I didn't know how involved I would be. I don't think the owners knew how involved I would be.

Everyone will always say that a restaurant is 'ambitious' when it opens, especially PR managers looking to pad out their media releases, but in my opinion, lending your energy and finances to a completely unregulated industry that is dependent on a system of labour exploitation and full of moving parts is already intrinsically ambitious. Add to that the fight against Melbourne rental prices, food costs, the fickle nature of diners and the fact that we have too many restaurants per person in the state, and even the most thoughtful and professional restaurant opening takes blind determination.

Being in my twenties, and having already worked in restaurants for five years, I naively believed that I knew how to anticipate things going wrong. But when the restaurant's general manager, a fifty-year-old front-of-house veteran we called Our Fearless Leader, cheerfully guaranteed that things would go wrong in every single way, I felt that anxiety of my childhood bubble up and settle in my lower intestine.

I was surprised that Our Fearless Leader was not a spring chicken (and due to the linear nature of time, is still not a spring chicken). After hitting their mid-thirties, hospo people usually took figurehead positions while they reared a litter of children, casting their eyes over the room once in a while and flitting about stroking the egos of regulars. Or they retired to the country and would bust through the venue without warning to say that everything was wrong and their legacy was being destroyed. But Our Fearless Leader was hands-on and had more energy than a teenager. He possessed an eye for detail that would inevitably cause him to injure himself chasing a speck of dust through the restaurant; he had no desire for children but would foster the growth of individuals within the businesses; he had no interest in getting a share in the restaurant but remained dedicated; and he really, really liked shoes. He also truly believed that everything would fall into place because, despite his experience, he was a blind optimist.

A dishevelled building was gutted. Dead possums were found under the floorboards wedged between the old beer lines. Floors were ripped out. Non-load-bearing walls were knocked down.

Concrete was cut to make way for new plumbing. New circuits were put in by electricians. Deliveries of stone, kitchen equipment and toilets arrived. Bars were put in. The space between the walls started to look more like a restaurant and less a like demolition site.

But this is where everything started to go wrong. Architects visited and argued with the builders for putting things in the wrong place. Circuits had to be moved or duplicated to accommodate equipment that required more energy to run than what was specified. Furniture would get stuck in customs. Natural stone was delivered cracked. The light fixtures would not look right once connected. The things that were meant to dim would not dim. Opening a restaurant always means being over budget and behind schedule.

Our Fearless Leader had to exude an air of positivity and confidence to allow everyone else around him to keep pushing through. He had the hard job of placating the owner, who was watching his bank account deplete while his 'ambitious' restaurant failed to take shape. Whenever we had a meeting to cover where things were at, in between the scatter-gun information Our Fearless Leader would offload on me, there was a lot of breath-holding, loud sighing and sarcastic laughter that made me think he was unravelling. Watching him calm down the management team, who had quit their previously high-paying jobs and were hanging out for full-time hours, was like watching a conman at work. He was literally having to talk the builders out of burying the hipster architects in concrete. His phone was always on speaker when he was extracting information from the chef, who had not yet arrived in Melbourne. I had no idea how he could figure out systems for a venue without a fleshed-out concept, or how he could time the hiring of staff when he was met with a new delay every day, but he did it all with a fake smile permanently plastered to his face.

It didn't matter that his smile was fake or if other people believed he was happy with the mess he agreed to stitch together. *He* believed it, and there was no stopping this train. In one of the few moments I caught him taking a breather from positivity, he told me to always allow an extra six weeks of build time to any restaurant. I looked at how much he emptied his tank for a project that he didn't even have ownership in and thought to myself that I would never do something as idiotic as opening my own restaurant. Nevertheless, I committed the six-week time frame to memory. You know, just in case.

Things were exactly six weeks behind by the time we hired staff and started the media push. Then our services started coming in – fridges, washers, stoves, fryers, freezers and all the ridiculous machines that make a restaurant work. I had a one-day, mind-numbing, classroom-style seminar on how to use the reservations system. Internally, like all restaurants, a few of us developed our own code so we could let each other know if the guest was a pain in the arse (*), was inappropriate with female waiters (FT, for Filthy

Toucher), would not always dine with their wife/husband (**),
preferred side tables (ST), liked bar seating (B), hated sitting at
the bar (NB) and if they tipped well (!). Surprisingly, it was one of
the first times I'd worked in a venue that didn't have a code for sex
workers (usually, this was to make sure that a junior staff member
didn't misread the situation and make it awkward). Everything
else, like allergies, was written out because life-threatening facts
couldn't be offensive and they're just something you can't afford to
fuck up.

Everything was a race to get the venue open as quickly and
cheaply as possible. We had already dealt with the fact that we
couldn't afford staff uniforms beyond aprons because we'd blown
the budget on the building. Heating was connected and we had
to settle on running it without the fan or risk blowing the light
fittings around the room.

And then I met the curious breed of humans who ran the
sanitary waste company. I did not expect them to be particularly
personable since their job was literally driving a combination of full
and empty bins filled with used pads and tampons around the city
and rotating them around in restaurants and office buildings, but
I thought they would at least introduce themselves. The woman
who was in charge of our account double-parked her truck outside
of the restaurant, dragged two empty bins behind her, barged in,
grunted, 'Where are the toilets?' at me, and kept walking through
the venue. The other managers were half an hour from arriving,

and she stopped in front of me with a slip of paper she expected me to sign to say she had performed her tampon bin delivery.

'Oh, we have three female toilets and a disabled toilet so we'll need two more bins,' I said, dangling my pen in the air, studying the piece of paper that confirmed we were missing bins.

'Don't have any more. You can have two today and I'll bring the other two tomorrow.' I didn't know that the number of bins we ordered was a suggestion.

'We're launching to a full restaurant tonight. Is there any way you can bring the other two bins today?'

'Not without me doing overtime.'

'I can't sign that to say you've delivered goods that you haven't delivered.'

'You can sign it tomorrow when I bring the other two.' She left.

When Our Fearless Leader arrived, I relayed the situation. 'It doesn't matter, there are two other bins that can be used,' was his male, confirmed bachelor response.

'I don't think you understand.'

'Oh, we'll be fine. It's the launch. How many people will need to use them in one night?'

'I don't think the volume is the issue,' I said, trying to explain the logistics of hygenically handling used sanitary items and that you can't just pass a bin under a stall like toilet paper.

Our Fearless Leader's smile made its first appearance of the day, and as if we were cosmically linked, my stomach bubbled.

'We'll be fine,' he said.

The hour before guests arrived, every single front-of-house staff member, including bartenders and sommeliers, assembled and ran through the proceedings of the night. After breaking up into our respective sections, I stood at the front desk with one of the junior managers Googling the names of all the guests we were expecting. They were a mix of socialites, inherently rich people and independently wealthy people. I knew exactly none of them.

Prior to this evening, I had only worked with Our Fearless Leader, but on this night, I met Senior Manager and Junior Manager. Senior Manager was also a little older, had previously worked as a manager in one of Melbourne's premier institution restaurants and possessed a cold and smug demeanour, along with a stellar reputation. I loved him immediately. Junior Manager had never held a management position in his life, came from a bar background, was only a few years older than me and seemed like he wanted to be everyone's friend. We were going to eat him alive.

People flooded in. The first obstacle when dealing with rich people is understanding that money doesn't always come with smarts. Take the common push-pull door to the restaurant, for example. There was a thirty per cent success rate with our launch night VIPs opening it correctly.

'There are only two options. If you can't pull it, push it, right?' I said to Junior Manager when a couple stood in front of the glass door with a prominent door handle expecting it to slide open like entering a lift.

'I guess we're getting a push sign,' said Senior Manager, raising one eyebrow at me. He replaced his smug expression with a warm smile, which, to me, looked fantastically condescending as he turned, pulled open the door and greeted the couple. 'Please, follow me,' he said, gesturing with one arm to seat them in the dining room.

'Mark off table twenty-five as seated,' he instructed when he came back to the host desk. I had the very easy job of meeting, greeting, running the reservations system and reporting back on errors on night one. As I checked off the table, a clock would appear over the guests' names, counting upwards so we would know how long they spent there. As the first wave of guests was seated, my job switched from greeting to monitoring.

In staff training, we aimed to get water to the table within a minute of guests being seated, a drink order two minutes after that, the drink to the table from three to seven minutes depending on what they ordered, a food order fifteen minutes after that, and their first dishes to arrive within six minutes of placing the order. We were running behind on everything. The very beautiful, sparkly people were all getting drunk quickly, cutlery was being knocked off tables and dishes were coming up on the pass but we didn't have enough people to run it out to the tables. Food would congeal, release oil, split or wilt under the heat lamps, and the kitchen would have to ditch the dead dishes and remake them to the standard of the head chef.

It took me twenty seconds to stomp from the host desk to the food pass at the rear of the restaurant, and on the way I would clear dishes, pour wines and run drinks with the goal of checking on how many dishes were left of the dockets of tables that needed turning. On my way back to the host desk, armed with new information, I would drop food to the appropriate tables before changing seating arrangements for the new wave of diners. My job was a glorified Musical Chairs. In my control-freak head, I told myself that if the next seating was taken to their tables without waiting, I won.

I turned the first few tables seamlessly and then I realised I was in the shit. Desserts were not getting out to the tables, and I ducked and weaved my way down to the kitchen to run plates out.

'We have an issue.'

'Yeah, I know we have an issue. I can't seat the second seating.'

'No, there's another issue,' said the head chef.

'Where are the food runners?' I asked.

'Bathroom. Female.'

Fuck.

I walked into the female toilets expecting to find a drunken guest passed out, or vomit, or a clogged toilet. Instead, I found two female food runners just standing in the middle of the bathroom staring into a stall.

'We don't know what to do about this, but we can't leave it,' said a runner. 'Like five people have already told us about it.'

There was a mountain of used tampons built up on the floor where the sanitary bin should have been, glowing red, almost congealing into a single solid mass from all the blood pooling together, oxidising to a terracotta brown and filling the unventilated room with the strong smell of dead, clotted, uterine lining.

Unlike in office jobs, hospitality workers are expected to do what needs to be done. My official job title may have been 'media manager and host', but it didn't preclude me from sticking my hand in the dishwasher to unclog it, washing and polishing stems, taking orders, setting tables, working the till, sweeping up cigarette butts or washing and scrubbing vomit outside the front of the restaurant. These poor runners, who were being underpaid more than I was being underpaid, were frozen with fear that they would have to glove up and dispose of Blood Mountain.

'Just run food. I'll deal with it.' The runners didn't even thank me as they ran back to the floor, probably too scared I'd change my mind.

Fucking gross bitches, I thought to myself. *I understand one drunk bitch putting her tampon on the floor, but why the hell did other people add to it? Everyone knows you wrap it up in toilet paper and throw it in the first bin you come across.*

I leaned out of the bathroom and grabbed a dirty spoon off a pile of plates someone was carrying to the kitchen. I stood in front of the stall, staring at the hill of blood-soaked cotton, and something in my brain clicked. My stomach stopped bubbling. I took a deep breath, stepped forward, extended my right leg, flexed my foot under the stall door and pulled it closed. I held the door shut with my foot as I used the spoon to turn the stall lock to 'closed', ditched it in the cutlery bucket and washed my hands.

This was way above my paygrade.

I returned to my station and sat the next wave of guests until I could chase down Our Fearless Leader, who had been in charge of fluffing all the VIPs this evening.

'Is everything all right?' he asked, when I managed to drag him to the front desk, pretending I needed his help with a table. I looked at the screen and pretended to click around.

'So, don't react when I tell you this.'

'You're acting like the building is on fire.'

'Remember when we only got two sanitary bins this afternoon?'

'Yes.'

'Remember when you said we would be fine?'

'What happened?'

'People have just been throwing their used tampons on the floor.'

Our Fearless Leader let out a tiny yelp at a frequency only dogs could hear.

'But don't worry,' I went on. 'I locked the door of the stall from the outside. I just don't think—'

Our Fearless Leader cut me off. 'Leave it. I'll call someone. I have someone for this. No staff member will ever clean faeces or things like *this* under my watch. If I can't stomach doing it, I won't make anyone else do it. Thanks for telling me. It will be sorted by the morning.'

He scurried off into the basement with his mobile and crept back up five minutes later. The rest of the night ran equally slow, but without the knot of anxiety in my gut. Once everyone left and we started to clean down, Senior Manager stood up at the host station with me to run through systems we needed to put in place or tweak.

'So, I heard about *the incident*.'

'Oh, yeah, it's fucking foul. Amazing behaviour by Melbourne's elite.'

'It's not the first time it's happened,' said Senior Manager.

'I thought you only worked in rich-people, fancy-pants restaurants before this.'

'You know what they say, you can't buy class but you can buy —'

'Cleaners?' I cut him off.

Senior Manager raised his eyebrow, shook his head and said, 'Blood bins.'

4

'Don't sit there,' said Michael the bartender. 'I watched Andy having sex on that couch on the security footage from last night. I'll never get the image of his bare arse bobbing up and down out of my mind.'

'Where hasn't Andy had sex in this bar?'

It was Christmas Eve and all the staff at The Restaurant decided to go for after-work drinks at the cocktail bar around the corner that was open until five in the morning. So, technically it was Christmas Day. Michael and Andy (not pub Andy, a different Andy) were always on the late shift at the bar, so our friendship revolved around them eating at The Restaurant before they started their shift, and us drinking at their bar when we ended ours. Since its hectic start, The Restaurant had lived up to all the owner's ambitions and become one of the city's go-to restaurants, and Michael had a goal of being the first person in Melbourne to eat through the entire forty-five item menu. It meant I saw him cry chilli tears several times a week. I'd always hand him extra napkins in preparation, before he even placed his order. That's how we started to bond.

'Yeah, good point. Just don't blame me if you end up with an STI.'

'I don't think I'll be rubbing my naked genitals anywhere on this couch. We should be fine.' It's disgusting, but I have dealt with a lot worse during service. Aside from the handsy couples who insist on sitting on the same side of the table, making everyone else uncomfortable as they try to swap tongues in front of their drinks before it is even eight o'clock, it's not uncommon to serve people who have a quickie and go for dinner without even splashing cold water on their faces afterwards. Good for them. I learned a long time ago that anything I wear at work is destined for a single wear and an extra-long spin cycle in the washing machine.

'Two wet gin martinis with a twist and three negronis?' It was Michael's favourite rhetorical question – he prided himself on knowing our drink orders before even we did. Though it's pretty difficult to say no to ninety millilitres of hard liquor over ice when you've just closed down a restaurant after a pre-public holiday dinner shift. The only day The Restaurant ever closed was Christmas Day, so we had to take extra care in making sure everything was perfectly tucked in for its annual twenty-four-hour sleep.

Senior Manager made a rule that we either worked Christmas Eve or New Years and that whoever was on close got the next day off. I knew I was going to get Christmas Day off regardless, but there was no way in hell I was going to work on the biggest shit show night of the year. I'd been with The Restaurant for almost a year and I was mostly on the floor during lunch service and making up office hours around it, but seeing as I was the only host without family commitments, I fell on my sword so other people could wrap presents, drink beers, eat cookies or whatever the hell families do on Christmas Eve.

I moved out of home when I was fifteen. Prior to that, my Christmases involved my sister and me being held hostage at our parents' Chinese Christian Baptist Church. My parents liked to cherry pick parts of their religion to suit their needs. God was the important part. The rituals involving gift-giving, spending time with your family and decoration were seen as a waste of time and money (plus my mother made every extended family gathering such a difficult experience that we were not invited to any other relatives' Christmases either). So instead, we were forced to sit in church and listen to everyone sing hymns in Chinglish, followed by an east-meets-west potluck. This is how I learned to hate fusion food. A lot of crimes have been committed by non-Chinese folk against Chinese food, but finding chunks of cold lap cheong in potato salad containing hidden raisins and cubes of apple made me want to call the police. I became known as a picky eater.

It was also no secret that I was agnostic. The thing my parents never considered when they pushed me to be an excellent student is that if you beat me into excelling at acquiring knowledge for practical (read: test) and recreational (read: social) purposes, my best friends would become books (no surprise that I wanted to be a writer) and I would inevitably discover philosophy. It was game over for me and religion before I even finished primary school, when I discovered Camus's *The Stranger* in the local library and tucked it into my bag next to my Hello Kitty thermos filled with herbal soup.

In my adult years, my friends took pity on me and I'd spend the day with their families. But this only forced me to face what I was lacking, and it always made me feel more isolated, even though – or especially because – I was surrounded by happy people. Seeing supportive, generous parents always made me feel uncomfortable. Being anything but on-edge around mothers just felt unnatural, like a joke was being played on me and the cruelty would come when I least expected it.

'So, what do you usually do for Christmas?' asked one of the section waiters who'd helped close that night. She was only on a single shift for the day, so had way more energy than the rest of us and drank her cocktails at the same speed I drank water. She directed the question to no one in particular, so everyone answered.

'Family.'

'Orphan's Christmas.'

'I go to my dad's then I go to my mum's.'

'I drink grower Champagne in my underwear in front of the television and watch the entire back catalogue of Lars von Trier films,' I responded.

'Oh, you can come to Orphan's with me if your family are all in Hong Kong,' said Jason, who was in Melbourne on a work visa from the UK.

'Nah, my family are here. Thanks, though.'

'So you don't see your family on Christmas when you have the day off?'

'I don't even speak to my family. They don't even know what I do.' I didn't allow them access to my life anymore.

'That's just weird,' said Jason. 'I love family Christmas. I love seeing my family, and watching my parents argue with my grandparents and overcook the roast. We swap really naff presents and then have a few too many of the beers my dad brews at home. It's so good.'

'The beer or the day?'

'Oh no, the beer is awful. I just miss my family and spending Christmas with them.'

'I have to see my mum and dad separately since they broke up,' Sarah said into her negroni.

'That's shit,' said Jason.

'Yeah, Mum was having an affair and then realised she's gay. Dad's remarried now. It's just weird 'cause both their new partners are named Lindsay.'

We all leaned in. Sarah was one of the food runners who often helped us clean down even if she'd clocked off. She usually tagged around for a drink. I understood her logic. If you go home and go to bed, tomorrow comes around a lot faster than you want it to.

'So, did your mum have an affair with her current partner?'

'No. She was going to therapy for a while 'cause Dad said she was just being really aggressive and distant. Her fortnightly appointments became weekly and the sessions went longer.'

'Was she boning her therapist?'

'No. She met someone in the waiting room and they'd go on coffee dates and stuff before or after her appointments and go back to her place.'

'Like in *The Sopranos!* When Tony hooks up with that absolutely mental chick!'

'That's what Dad said when she told him. Then he said he hoped her new girlfriend was as psycho as that character from *The Sopranos*. It actually turned out that she had a problem committing and blew up my parents' marriage for no reason. But that's how Mum realised she likes women. That's why I see Dad first, 'cause otherwise he sits at the table asking questions about Mum the whole time. He doesn't believe she's actually gay. Then his new wife gets all passive aggressive with me because she thinks he should be over it by now, but she's also just with him for the money anyways, so yeah.'

'Underwear. Television. Champagne. I can't recommend it highly enough.'

'I would be disowned!'

'Christmas is meant to be a shitshow. You can't just bow out of it,' said Andy, the only one of us actually spending the day with his whole family at the same time. 'You're supposed to be miserable and drunk all day and then get into a fight with your siblings. I only see my brother once a year and that's Christmas Day. He sucks.'

I'd never been into family drama because my own family were so secretive. I didn't know how my parents met, what their hopes or dreams were, why they chose to move to Australia even though my dad's side chose San Francisco, or anything about their past – and it was considered taboo for my sister and I to ask. Everything I knew about them was purely observational. Very little of it was good. Aside from being discouraged from asking for context, I was afraid of what I would find out. So I avoided it. Maybe it was the long shift serving tourists on holiday, maybe it was forgetting to eat dinner, maybe it was the goblet of cold gin I'd thrown back in three gulps, but to my own surprise, I asked Andy, 'Why does he suck so hard?'

'Well, he had a drug problem and kept stealing money from my parents. When they hid their money too well, he chased them around with a baseball bat, stole their surround-sound system – as in, fully ripped it out of the wall – watches, whatever was worth anything, and pawned it all for cash. I let him live with me for a while, but it turned out he was stealing from me, too. I'm just over it. And now, he's apparently sober and rich but he's still an arsehole.'

'You can't forgive him?'

'You're supposed to apologise to everyone as part of the twelve steps, but he hasn't apologised to me. So he can get fucked.'

This was the moment I realised I loved gossip. I had been starved of it all my life. That evening, I learned which of my colleagues had 'fished off the company pier', which of them had broken up, even though I didn't know they were dating, and which regulars were crazy stalkers. I didn't know what was fact, what was rumour and what was speculation, but I lapped it up like a kitten at a saucer full of milk.

As the night wore on and the effects of chilled liquor impaired our judgement, arguments broke out. Sarah had a bone to pick with Jason because she heard that he slept with someone else at work the night after they went on a date. Andy was pissed off at Sarah for telling someone about him getting all emotional about his family when they got drunk together on their days off. And I learned that as sweet and delicious as gossip is, it is best not to spread it or be part of it. I loved hearing it, but I would become a vault.

In the new year, people began to come to me to freak out about the itch they felt in their crotch, help them work out their cycle to figure out how late they were, or ask me to buy them underpants and a toothbrush from Target on the way to work because they hadn't been home since the day before. People trusted me with their secrets because I kept them and told them hard truths to their faces instead of behind their backs. I would act surprised at the scandal involving a married chef, the beautiful new section waiter and a bartender; and feign shock at the revelation that every second staff member had chlamydia. We liked to use the phrase 'fish off the company pier' to describe staff members who hooked up, but my incredibly literal mind could never get past the image of a mammal and a fish smashing nether regions.

Eventually, all the staff drama just became the same plot lines recycled with different people and I lost interest. It was when regulars or drunk guests offered up ridiculous stories that my vault got filled with fresh, gossipy treasure.

There was one older gentleman who liked to sit at the bar and flirt with everyone. His first name rhymed with his surname, so for the purpose of storytelling, I'll refer to him as Ronald McDonald. Ronald McDonald was bald, short and had a love of sweet cocktails. He'd wink at every person we sat on either side of him, and ingratiated himself with the bar boys to see if he could massage them out of their training for a cheeky, heavier pour. He was impossibly nice to the floor staff, so any dishes that were accidentally made would end up in front of him as a free snack. Ronald McDonald knew how to be a regular.

He was also very loose-lipped.

One night, before we moved him along, he told me he was being bad because he'd just eaten a stack of meat and chased it with a handful of cocktails while recovering from a gout flare-up. He put his weight on my shoulder to get off the stool and hobbled off into the night. Another evening, he told me he'd never properly worked in his life because of his inheritance and didn't know how people could drag themselves to their jobs every day. (I tried to explain the concept of being poor to him, but he just nodded along, unable to actually fathom it.) Finally, whenever we let him finish his last drink as we packed down around him (we'd got to treating him a bit like furniture, he was there so often), he told us that when he was a young man he'd had such drawn-out, sugar-daddy-type affairs with various members of federal parliament that he was surprised they were even straight-presenting today. He shared details about what each person was into, what they bought him, who was the most aggressive about being closeted and why he eventually had to move to Melbourne to get away from them. He also used the phrase 'cauliflower arsehole' so many times that I couldn't eat cauliflower for the next six months. It was on that night that he chose to give me his credit card to pay for the bill and I noticed the name on the card wasn't his.

'Ronald, is this your card?'

'Yes, dear.'

'This isn't your name.'

'Oh, it's my parents' card. I'm on it. Check the last name.'

'I thought you said you got a huge inheritance.'

'Yes, and I am spending it while they're alive.'

'When your parents are still alive, I believe it's just called an allowance.'

Ronald howled at that comment and tipped generously. 'Seventy years old and with an allowance. I suppose you're right.' And he giggled his way out to the street.

The lie that all forms of media have told about working in restaurants is that restaurant workers are well fed with good food. In my experience, very few venues have fed me well – if at all. One of the most disgusting staff meals I ever had to choke down was offcuts of pork that were mostly fat and not fully cooked, premixed into a soggy salad that was dressed with apple juice and English mustard. There wasn't a lick of salt to the meal and it was dumped on top of hard, undercooked rice, a grain of which lodged itself between my back teeth and annoyed me all evening until I got home and flossed. As a bonus, I also ended up with a stomach ache for the next few days. At the same venue, on the complete other spectrum of staff meals, a different chef took the time and care to serve us mul naengmyeon, a Korean noodle dish served in a chilled soup, on a forty-degree day when the air conditioning was struggling and we were all crunching on ice and ruining our enamel to get through the night.

At The Restaurant, every single meal was chicken wings. They'd be fried, they'd end up in tom yum soup, they'd find their way into a jungle curry. We'd have chicken wings in massaman instead of beef (do not recommend). I imagined a factory full of amputee hens, struggling to find their centre of balance. It wasn't horrible, but after you eat chicken wings a couple of times in a row, you don't want to see another wing again. And even though we worked our arses off, every single staff member would put on weight very quickly and their sudden change in shape would result in a lack of spatial awareness. Eventually, everyone started picking around the protein and we'd fill all the waiters' stations with crackers, lollies and jerky.

This could explain why between 2.30 and 4pm, the bar at The Restaurant was always full of hospo workers looking for a quick meal before going back to their own venues. On one particular day, half of our front-of-house team had been taken down by the flu, so I switched between seating people and filling in wherever a set of hands was needed. The entire bar was stacked with dirty glassware after the lunch rush, so I assigned myself as dish bitch, allowing Evan, the lone barman of the day, to restock and prep for another short-staffed service. A group of workers from a flashy, high-end, nationally franchised restaurant came in for the meal that hospo workers have between what regular people might call lunch and dinner – but which is technically their breakfast. At the bar, I was in the perfect position to eavesdrop.

'I begged one of the chefs to serve up the raft he was using to clarify stock as staffy and he said no. They were gonna share it in the kitchen,' said one of guys at the bar, loosening his tie. Bleak. As I listened in, I shifted closer to the group.

'Yesterday, we had a vegetable stew that the chef forgot about, so it was like eating a homogenised ball of clag with burned bits stirred through it. I don't know if that made it better or worse, because they gave the whole thing texture, but it was bitter as hell.' This worker stuck out his tongue and fake-gagged as emphasis.

'Yeah, well, you weren't there for the eggplant curry that someone made where the eggplant was raw and the spices weren't cooked off. It's a talent to make a vegetable taste like leather,' said one of his friends.

These meals sounded like they were crafted by high-school home economics students rather than a brigade of hardcore, macho, flame-controlling, tough-nuts who prided themselves on their roles as chefs at a prestigious venue.

'I just don't understand how you can want to be a chef and serve shit for a staff meal,' one of the visiting waiters continued. 'They just don't give a fuck. We make them coffees, we give them their knock offs. Some reciprocation would be nice.'

'Don't you work in one of the best restaurants in the state?' asked Evan, The Restaurant's naïve daytime bartender who thought chicken wings every day was the apex of luxury.

'According to the boring food writers who come in for freebies off the back of the PR team. It's the only time our Big Name Chef graces us with his presence, and then he makes a huge mess that we have to clean up.'

'Where is he if he's not cooking?'

'Well, he's just going around smiling like an idiot and cheating on his wife all over the country.' The door to my gossip vault swung open, ready to receive more goods. I turned my body away from the group, trying to look focused on the lip of the wine glass I was polishing.

One of the crew leaned in towards his friends. 'Did you hear about Thailand? He goes every year and stimulates the economy with his love of young men.'

'No way. What is your proof?'

'Our manager told us.'

'He hit on me,' said the only woman in the group.

'He hits on every single female. Though you are his type. Asian.'

She recoiled at his comment and put her fork down on her plate, turning her energy inwards and staring into space.

'Hey, I didn't mean to upset you. Are you all right?'

She didn't say anything for a while, and her colleagues looked at Evan and me in a panic. I kept polishing and Evan kept prepping. I told myself to stay out of this one. Evan, with his big, beautiful heart, decided to break the silence and ask her what happened.

'You don't have to tell me if you don't want to, but if you want to get it off your chest, we're here for you.' Fool. Even a gossip lover like me knew there were some stories you're better off not knowing.

'It was when I started. He was down for one of his media lunches and he just walked up to me and asked me if I'd be interested in being his Melbourne girlfriend. He didn't even ask me what my name is, or what I do in the company. He didn't introduce himself, he just assumed I knew who he was. He told me he would put me up in an apartment and take care of me, but when he was in Melbourne, he'd have to stay with me. He put his hand on my waist and then kissed me on the cheek. He said he'd get my response the next day, but thankfully, it was my day off.'

The boys sat there staring at her with their mouths wide open. Eventually one finally managed to talk. 'That's fucked. Did you tell HR?' Such a male response.

'You mean HR that makes us work sixty-hour weeks and doesn't pay us outside of our contracted thirty-eight hours?' Silence.

'Hey, Jess.' It was Senior Manager. 'Can you work for a bit tonight? Tonight's host also has the flu. I'll let you go early because I know you've been here since nine, but there is no one else to do the door with me.'

'Yeah, I've got nowhere to be.'

'Go on break. Come back in an hour.'

'I'll finish these glasses first 'cause Ev's got no one else in the bar until briefing.' Deep down, I wanted to hear the woman tell her colleagues the realities of being a sexually harassed woman in hospitality.

'One of the runners just came back from break. I'll make him do it. See you in an hour.'

On my way out of the bar, I looked at the woman who'd just unpacked a large source of trauma related to the space she spent more time in than her own home. She caught my eye, and we exchanged a helpless and fed-up look of acknowledgement. I thought of past managers attempting to groom me, owners calling me hot like I wasn't in the room, all the bathrooms in bars I'd been assaulted in by drunken colleagues. These experiences weren't unique to me. I wasn't special. I'd told no one, but they were open secrets. Nothing was going to change.

The woman's colleagues had already forgotten about it and were finishing the food on their plates in silence. She would go back to work the next day terrified of Big Name Chef making an appearance. Meanwhile, in the best-case scenario her experience would be swept under the rug. It was just as possible that it would be spread around and questioned until the crushing weight of gossip forced her to resign. She stabbed at her plate and ate enough to avoid having to dip into her staff meal, and I thought about my own.

I checked the time at the front desk, grabbed my wallet and ran out the door. There would be no chicken wings, jerky, crackers or lollies for me that evening. I did some quick calculations. If I power-walked, I could order an awesome bowl of noodles and be back in time for briefing. If I strolled, I could grab a baguette and a glass of wine somewhere mediocre but sufficient before I needed to head back. If I ran, I could have a quick shower, reheat some leftovers, save some money and get back to work not feeling greasy. I chose the option with the glass of wine.

At a nearby cafe I ordered the last baguette in the display window. The rare roast beef had spent the entire afternoon bleeding into the bread, turning the interior soggy in all the wrong places. It was too dry and too wet at the same time, but I was grateful that I wasn't eating some iteration of wings. Plus, the cheap house red served to me in a latte glass, which was predominantly shiraz, helped wash it down. As I was brushing the crumbs off me, my phone pinged. It was Christina, a uni friend who had also abandoned her creative pursuits. She'd recently been off again with her on-and-off-again loser boyfriend who was nice to her maybe once every cycle of their relationship. There was a group of us who always tried to knock some sense into her, but we had been unsuccessful for years. She was in the reckless phase of the breakup, which usually came before the revenge phase, just before she pulled into jealousy junction and decided to sacrifice her vagina to prevent some poor woman from being fooled by her ex. The text read: 'Drinks. Tonight.'

I responded with, 'Can't. Working.'

She fired back to me with, 'I'm coming in. Need to see you.' I didn't respond. At least we had an endless supply of very soft three-ply napkins available at work. They were excellent for mopping up spills and emotions. I checked the time, threw back the last third of my glass of wine, paid and walked back to The Restaurant. I tossed my wallet and phone into the host desk and Senior Manager pulled up next to me.

'Do you see who's on fifteen?'

I took a quick glance and immediately recognised one of the tanned, blonde, men-children man-spreading across several tables in the centre of the restaurant.

'Yep.'

'Do you know him?' Senior Manager was under the impression that I knew everyone under the age of forty even though I knew no one. But I did recognise the person he was referring to. He was the only person at the table with a profile, a guy who was regularly featured in The Daily Mail thanks to his recklessness with money and women. He was, and still is to this day (surprisingly), inherently rich. He also fell under the category of Hot Idiot: good for now, bad for your list of life regrets.

'Nope,' I lied. We'd met the last time he was in Melbourne, when he was eating his way through every restaurant that had opened up since his last bacchanalian adventure in the city. Someone on his table saw me being chummy with the staff in the restaurant while I was eating and recognised me through social media. They made the strange assumption that I must be someone worth knowing. Hot Idiot spent the next few hours crashing my dinner to show me videos of him swimming with dolphins, then tried to get me to take him and his friends for drinks afterwards. I did not.

Seeing him there now, I turned my energy down and hoped he wouldn't recognise me, but how many Cantonese chicks with a shaved head and platinum-blonde fuzz work in hospitality?

'Anything I need to know that happened in the last hour?' I asked Senior Manager.

'We're still out of the same things. No specials. I wrote who is in what section for you on that piece of paper. Just look after the door while I do the briefing for pre-shift,' said Senior Manager.

'Easy.'

Christina walked through the door and hugged me so tightly she squeezed the air out of my lungs. She smelled like she'd already had a few drinks.

'Do you mind if I seat you at the bar?' I asked.

'I *want* you to seat me at the bar. Then I can hit on any hot men.' I was wrong. She'd graduated from the reckless phase into the revenge phase. I grabbed a drinks list and sat her in the dead centre of the bar. That way, she'd have the undivided attention of bartender Evan, and the confirmation that no one hot was dining.

'Princess,' said a voice behind me.

'I think you already know someone,' I said to Christina.

'It's not me they know,' she said. I turned around. It was him. Of course he'd forgotten my name.

'Princess, remember me?'

'My name is Jess.'

'Do you remember me?' He said, opening up his body for a hug. I stood there with my arms by my side, staring at him until he got the hint.

'Yes, John. I remember you.'

'Have a seat with us. We're having a late lunch.'

'Can't. I'm working.'

'I'm not,' said Christina, introducing herself with an extended hand.

I left them to get on with my job, then turned to see Christina walking with John to his table in the middle of the restaurant. He dragged over a chair from another table and made sure Christina slid in close to him. As soon as she let out her first fake laugh, I knew I would not be having an early night.

'Princess, hey,' said Senior Manager, back from briefing.

'Don't even.'

'I thought you said you didn't know him.'

'Who *really* knows anybody ...'

'Did he?'

'Yep.'

'Did you?'

'Nope.'

'Smart.' I could feel the eyeballs of my colleagues burning questions into the back of my head, and for the first time, I knew what it felt like to be the one at the centre of speculation. For a dinner shift, we were relatively quiet, and by eight-thirty, Senior Manager told me to get ready to clock off. He also motioned towards Christina, whose eyes were now pointing in different directions despite the double serve of carb-heavy corn fritters and chilli jam she'd eaten. She kept picking up other people's phones from the table to take selfies, mistaking them for her own. John's friends all played along and posed with her, smiling for a brief moment before retuning their attention to their plates, picking at soft shell crab and noodles drenched in sweet soy.

'You better take care of your friend before you come in bright and early tomorrow at nine.'

I let out a soft groan, grabbed my things from the host desk and walked over to Christina.

'Hey, do you want to share a taxi with me?' I asked.

'We are going out!'

'Don't you have to work tomorrow?'

'I can chuck a sickie. Who cares? Let's have fuuuuuuun.' I may have been friends with Christina since uni, but she clearly didn't know my definition of fun.

'One drink,' said John, with his smarmy face hanging off Christina's shoulder. I imagined all the phone calls I'd get from Christina tomorrow asking me if I remembered anything from the night, and chastising me for letting her be irresponsible with her vagina again. I weighed up the pain of dealing with a hysterical, regretful, recently dumped friend versus enduring (definitely) more than one drink with a recently dumped friend and coaxing her to make good decisions around a cashed-up fuck boi who would probably give her a parting gift of itchy lips. I decided that a late night would be getting off lightly.

As I dragged Christina out of the venue, Senior Manager gave me eyes that said, *I know who I'd rather not be right now*, but his mouth said, 'Thanks for coming, have a nice evening.'

By the weight Christina was putting on me to get out the front door, I figured she had a maximum of two drinks left in her. The combination of dark spirits and white wine seeping out of her pores, along with the high-sugar foods she'd eaten for dinner, suggested she would be throwing up tomorrow and asking me why I'd let her drink so much. A much better outcome than the potential flurry of paranoid texts she could be sending me from pathology while awaiting a sexual health test.

'Where are we going?' I asked.

'Not far,' said John. I realised his hanger-oners didn't speak. They just nodded, grunted and helped him finish off whatever food was left on the table after he had his one bite from each plate, but they didn't drink. Even though they all had the same look – sun-bleached locks, crushed linen shirts and shoes-without-socks – John was built like a sprinter, while his lackeys were as wide as they were tall. It became obvious to me that John had no friends. He had bodyguards that posed as his friends. It must be a lonely life being a rich, hot idiot.

Christina was starting to fade. Her steps became more dragged out, and every time we passed a bar, she'd pivot her body towards it and say, 'What about here?' It was clear John had no intention of going to the closest bar to The Restaurant, and I was slowly dragging Christina in the opposite direction to both our homes.

Eventually John finally stopped. 'Here we are.'

Oh, fuck no. We were standing outside the casino. And before midnight, too – that was the behaviour of a real gambling addict. I have always had a strong aversion to casinos because both my grandfathers were addicted to gambling. My paternal grandfather somehow gave up drinking and smoking, but gambling was his maladaptive coping strategy to deal with my grandmother leaving him. Every time we hung out, he'd drag me through the casino and all the security guards would introduce themselves to me and shake his hand or wave hello to him. I learned that the only words he knew in English were 'chips', 'again' and 'cash out'.

John led us through the entrance, past the high-end fashion stores with impeccable lighting, past the expensive-but-mostly-shit restaurants, and to the second floor that I had never been to. We were standing outside the Mahogany Room. John sweet-talked the receptionist into letting his entourage, Christina and me in with him because it was empty.

'Do you have your card, sir?' John threw down his Amex Black and she swiped it. 'It appears you have ten thousand dollars in uncollected winnings from your last visit. Would you like us to use that credit for your visit today?'

'Sure.'

I threw up in my mouth a little. I'd never had ten thousand dollars in my bank account before, let alone forgotten ten thousand dollars somewhere in a city I didn't live in. I guess being lonely is fine when you're this rich.

We walked through to the very exclusive high-roller gambling den and I was immediately disoriented by the not-quite-day-time-not-quite-night-time lighting. Everything smelled of stale cigarettes and depression.

'Can I get you anything to eat or drink?' A waiter popped out of nowhere. I looked at Christina and her half-open eyes and said, 'Could we please get a couple of glasses of water?'

'Oh, us, too.' The henchmen speak.

'I've got an idea,' said John, 'How about I give you a grand, two grand or whatever, and you can play whatever you want. You can keep your winnings, I just want my money back. Deal?' I didn't get a chance to say anything before John started distributing chips. He firmly pressed two one-thousand-dollar chips into my hand and disappeared into the levels of despair.

Our drinks arrived, and instead of participating in the most addictive sport of my people, I sat with John's sober bodyguards and uncomfortably sipped my water while trying to force Christina to down hers.

'Stop it! I'm going to the bathroom.' She stood up and looked at me, waiting.

'I'm not coming with you. I'm sure you can manage by yourself.'

'I don't know where it is.'

'Ask someone.'

Christina stormed off and wove around the tables with the chips in her hand. While she was gone, I tried to have a conversation with the rest of the table, but they were too involved with their phones.

'Are any of you going to gamble?'

'Nah, I did once and lost it all. I had to pay him back within twenty-four hours. I've learned my lesson.' The henchman didn't even look up at me when he spoke. We sat in silence for ten minutes, or ten hours, I couldn't tell.

'I'm going to go check on Christina.' The waiter who took our water order came to our table to ask if he could get anything else for us, and he showed me where the toilet was with a swift wave of his right arm. I prepared myself for a session of holding back hair and offering words of encouragement, but when I opened the door of the bathroom, I found a pristine facility with nobody inside. I checked the stalls, and the toilet rolls still had their crisp, V-shape folds. Christina never made it. I walked back onto the gambling-room floor and asked the waiter if he'd seen my friend. I asked the henchmen and they shook their heads. I asked the croupiers and they were no help.

I texted Christina. 'Where the fuck are you?' As I waited for the tell-tale dots to appear on the screen, I did a last scan of the room and walked up to John. He was playing blackjack and had amassed a huge collection of one-thousand-dollar chips in front of him.

'Hey, do you want a go?' he asked.

'No. I'm looking for Christina. Have you seen her?'

'I've just been concentrating on the game I'm playing with Roger here. Sorry.' I could count at least thirty thousand in chips next to John's inch of whisky. 'But I've lost the last few games, so I think I might move on.'

'Yeah, I'm going to go find Christina.' I set his two chips down next to him and gave them a double tap for emphasis.

'Well, at least say goodbye,' John said. Then he looked at Roger. 'Good to see you again.'

'You too, sir.'

'Out of curiosity, what's the largest tip you've ever received?' John asked.

'That would be one thousand dollars, sir.'

John looked up at me and slid the two thousand I'd set down next to him towards Roger.

'Thank you, that's very generous of you,' Roger said.

'So, this is now the largest tip you've ever received?'

'Yes, sir.'

'Out of curiosity, who was the person who tipped you one thousand?'

'That would be you, sir.'

I held back my laugh. 'Bye, John, I have to go. I'm working tomorrow.'

'See ya, Princess,' he said, standing up and enveloping me in a whisky-soaked hug.

'Don't call me Princess.'

I walked out into the street and my phone pinged. Christina. 'Couldn't find toilet. Went home to pee.'

As I walked back through the city, I cackled with laughter so loudly that people started staring at me. I didn't care. Christina was going to wake up one dick short of revenge, but two thousand dollars up in schadenfreude.

5

Early mornings and late nights became normal for me. Before I straddled a role that was half-office and half-floor as the media manager and host at The Restaurant, I'd worked late mornings and late nights, which seemed reasonable despite the workday still consisting of four more hours than an office worker's. At other times I'd juggled a part-time day job with night shifts, or worked around a university timetable. This, I told myself, was the first time I would have a consistent routine. I'd been with The Restaurant for eighteen months by this stage, and it was probably the longest I'd stayed at any job so far.

Back when I worked at the pub and decided to quit smoking, I'd taken up Muay Thai to transfer my nervous energy into something else. My logic was that if my lungs were being strained to the point of bursting, filling them up with any more tar would kill me. Plus, I couldn't afford both the classes and the cigarettes on a restaurant wage. It was an extreme but effective trade. My addiction went from rolling up tobacco and looking like a dickhead to spending my mornings throwing punches, kicks and elbows and looking like a dickhead. It was the only thing I did for myself, so it became my one non-negotiable activity of the day. I'd scrape myself out of bed no matter how much I didn't want to, so I could start my day with a type of physical and mental exertion that had nothing to do with the restaurant world. It was my measuring stick of trashbaggery. I rationalised that if I spent an hour keeping up with these fighters, I couldn't possibly be as gross or directionless as everyone else around me. It also meant I was never late for work.

For months we were short-staffed and I didn't have a day off. My weekdays consisted of waking up at 5.45am, catching a tram to the city, training, showering in a gross locker room, lugging my training gear up a hill to open The Restaurant at a quarter to nine, working on media and marketing, accepting deliveries, making sure all the front of house crew were in on time, calling around to find a replacement for anyone who was sick, doing lunch service, break, coming back for dinner service, drinking until I felt like I could go to bed, walking home and sleeping. On the weekends I had mornings off but came in for dinner service and would always make my way home via a bar. I ended up conceding to my timetable, realising my hours were unliveable in a share house where everyone worked nine-to-five, and moving into a one-bedder in the city where I could give myself an extra forty-five minutes of sleep every day.

The routine was absurd, but it was also reliably constant. Even though I was one of the youngest employees in The Restaurant, I somehow snagged myself an executive position. I was in charge of a department (though, granted, still didn't have people who reported to me yet) and had to sit in meetings with other department heads to work out how to make everything run like a well-oiled machine. I'd always thought I'd keep going with hospitality until I figured out how to make money from my creative arts degree. I'd never intended it to be my career, but I was now a fully integrated professional plate-carrier who rarely read and forgot about writing altogether.

On the organisational chart, I sat alongside front-of-house veterans who'd spent half a century roaming the earth, chefs who had worked overseas under famous chefs, and managers who'd had long careers in highly awarded Melbourne restaurants where mains started at fifty dollars a plate. I was also the only female. I did not feel like I belonged. But I had never felt like I belonged. At least while in this state of not belonging, I held a respectable position in a role I created for myself and was, for the first time ever, paid entitelements. I told myself that if I couldn't handle this, I should probably go find myself a desk job and shrivel up with all the other lemmings.

The reality was, I knew I had made myself unemployable in any other setting.

I was young and impressionable, but being the oldest I had ever been, I refused to believe I was in fact young and impressionable. I spent the mornings in meetings with all the big-tops and the owner, who would communicate effectively but not professionally. In the space of a few months, our morning meetings would undo all the tertiary education brainwashing that told me I had to speak respectfully and neutrally to get my point across. This is not the case in hospitality. We would sit in the room and say that the numbers were shit one day and fucking great the next. We would point the finger at the person who fucked up the week before and go back to our individual tasks. There was no such thing as neutral language and constructive criticism in hospitality. No one had time for that shit, especially the owner. My afternoons were spent arm-in-arm with front-of-house staff whose only common language of understanding was flirtation, and a brigade of crass chefs intent on flexing their masculinity or flaunting their homosexuality. I was dropping f-bombs and the c-word like it was punctuation and escalating inappropriate jokes to the point where I would make chefs blush. And I was proud of it. Despite my education, skills and ability, I made myself an HR nightmare.

But I was overrun. Hosting was a two-person job: you needed one host to manage the endless line of excited and irritated diners, and another to seat people at their tables. The original plan had been to have the managers work as hosts alongside me, but The Restaurant was so much busier than we'd predicted that they were too busy dealing with complaints or cashing out bills.

We needed to hire another person.

People would come in and interview, but once they saw the line at the door and every single staff member literally running on the restaurant floor, they ended the interview early, thanked Senior Manager for his time, said the role wasn't for them and ran out of the building, in case we asked them to trial on the spot.

It took a few months, but finally, we managed to hire someone: the girlfriend of Senior Bar Manager, who was finishing up study and had extensive experience working in restaurants. She already knew the crew through her boyfriend and was under no illusion that the job was cruisy since she'd listened to us bitch so much. She even asked for evening shifts so she'd have a similar schedule to her boyfriend. I liked her because I thought she was intelligent and savage, but I loved her when I found out she was giving me my nights and weekends back.

The first afternoon after I handed over to new Night Host, I slung my bag over my shoulder, left the building and was at a loss for what to do with all this extra time. I was used to gliding through empty streets in a hypnotic trance, smelling of food I did not eat, covered in a light film of sweat and chanting for booze like zombies did for brains.

I stood on the corner like a directionless idiot and imagined all the awkward first dates where the couple would be too polite to order anything, wasting an entire table for thirty dollars' worth of drinks and not leaving a tip. I envisioned all the women meeting in groups for their ladies' nights, woo-hoo-ing over nothing, trying to alter half the dishes on the menu to contain as few calories as possible then complaining that their requested food was bland. I pictured the groups of bros charging through drinks and hitting on anyone young and female – including me, even though I looked like a prepubescent boy. I pictured tourists rolling into venues without having researched them and being met with the great 'no bookings' trend of Melbourne, expecting us lowly antipodeans to roll out the red carpet for someone who happened to get on a plane for longer than eight hours, complaining about everything from the low lighting to the high volume of the overly trendy playlist, wondering why alcohol was so expensive and responsibly measured, and vowing never to come to the most liveable city in the world again. I could hear the single most used and least effective line ever dropped in public: 'Don't you know who I am?' My solution to being asked that question was to always stand there with an expression that said *yes, I am this simple*, and respond with, 'No, I'm sorry. I don't.' Then I'd wait for the self-important person to feel small. The truth is, I always knew who the person was because it was my job to know, but I call these Bimbo Rights: treat me like a dumb door bitch and you'll receive the dumb-door-bitch treatment. I just had to keep telling myself this job was for now, and not forever. I was financially stable for the first time in my life, but I did not feel fulfilled. I was numb, dumb and trapped by security and routine. I needed to do something creative again.

Anything. Something. It had been a long time since I allowed myself to turn my thoughts inwards.

I gave myself a shake and left the corner, cutting through the sea of people imitating John Brack's *Collins St., 5pm* until I got to my apartment. Then I sat in that near-empty white box with its cliched fridge full of condiments and my last inch of gin. I threw my stanky gym gear in the wash and listened to it tumble. I had a shower, sat on my couch, twiddled my thumbs and watched the sky turn from amber to black from the fifteenth floor. It was barely eight o'clock, and I was bored. I didn't have a television to turn on because up until this day, I hadn't needed one. As I sat there coming to terms with how empty my apartment was, I realised I didn't really live in it. It was just a space I slept in. I didn't come home to a family or have housemates to distract me. There was no one tinkering in the kitchen to have a conversation with. There was no one who wanted to grab a pub meal, or who might require consultation on whether they looked like they were trying too hard for a first date. I had no idea how to live alone, even though I'd spent my whole life striving for personal space.

I opened the door to my balcony and listened to the chatter of voices below me, the gentle whir of car engines crawling the length of a city block, endless clanking from construction, dings from trams, bells from food delivery bikes and the hum of extraction fans pulling fumes into the atmosphere. Behind these sounds, the city seemed suspiciously quiet. I didn't move to the city for quiet.

What the hell did normal people do when they came home from work? Everything I could think of – pets, children, hobbies, dinner parties, AA – involved responsibility or being part of a community, and neither of those things were for me. I lacked the empathy required to keep an animal alive and I didn't have the emotional range to make meaningful relationships with other people. I opened my box of notebooks from university and looked for ideas worth expanding on. I grabbed a new notebook so I could jot down ideas. I stared at the blank page for an excruitiating amount of time and ended up drawing a box in the top-right-hand corner and colouring it in solid black with a fine-tipped ballpoint pen.

I checked my phone for the hundredth time. The Restaurant would be heaving by now. I heard a faint ringing in my ears. It wasn't tinnitus – it was the absence of a commercial-grade speaker directly above me blasting overproduced hipster music while people shouted their names and numbers in my ear. Even when I left the host desk, I was always in a noisy bar, yelling over the music to have meaningless conversation with my friends while filling my head with liquid. By the time I left, I would be successfully anaesthetised. The ringing wasn't my body warning me about potential hearing damage (though it was also doing that), it was my body recognising that for the first time in months, I was about to be left alone with my thoughts. No, thank you.

I knew everyone's roster, so I texted the people I knew had the night off. They all had plans: on a date, seeing a movie, studying for an exam, at the gym, or moving house. It was mid week, so I didn't bother contacting my friends who worked regular jobs. If they were out, they'd be trying to get their genitals wet. My friends who were shift workers were unfortunately working. Fuck it. I'd be a lone wolf.

I never felt any anxiety about being a lone diner. My a job had already put me on the lowest rung of the social ladder, and I was under no illusion that I was important or interesting enough for people to point out and speculate about my solitary status. I also didn't have the concerns that many women have about going out on their own – if my platinum-blonde buzzcut didn't make me seem sexually ambiguous enough, my self-imposed uniform made me look perpetually prepared for a zombie apocalypse. I looked practical but not approachable.

I got dressed, jammed some headphones in my ears and left my apartment. I wandered around Chinatown listening to the Sugarcubes, hoping Bjork's punk-pop trills, squeals and sighs would be the antidote to the tinny autotune earworm crawling around in my brain. I was sniffing out dinner, but I wasn't hungry. My body wasn't used to being hungry at a reasonable hour, even though my brain knew it should be eating. I walked up and down the hill from Spring Street to Swanston, taking the scenic route by meandering through the side streets until I ended up at one of the bars we would go to for knock-offs.

It was empty.

It wasn't just empty, it was well lit and didn't smell of sweat, vinegared breaths and liquor. There weren't piles of backpacks filled with dirty aprons, pens and filthy uniforms shoved into every corner of the room. The bartenders looked fresh and were taking turns sitting down to a vegetable-based dinner comprised of more than three colours.

'Hey, what are you doing here this early, did you get fired?' one of thebartenders asked.

'Ha. Finally hired another host. I get nights off and an actual weekend, now.'

'Time for a celebratory shot, then.'

It was the first shot of the night. It felt wrong doing one in a hospo bar without other hospo people, but that didn't stop me from having more. It was the first time I'd actually got to see the bar properly. I learned that it had a list of house cocktails. I also realised I had been calling both the bartenders the wrong names, but they were always too in the weeds to correct me.

As the night wore on, staff from other late-night hospo bars would pop in for their half-hour breaks and nurse their woes before heading back to push through until sunrise. These people were the real mercenaries of the hospo scene. They were our saviours. They had to put up with us after we'd put up with the general public. They had the highest tolerance level of anyone in the industry. They were the ultimate Night Walkers. I bought them shots from across the room and nodded at them in acknowledgement.

Staff from nearby restaurants started to arrive, ditch their bags in corners and hold tables for their friends. People always asked me how I knew everyone even though I worked at the same time everyone else was working. This was how: knock-offs. We may not have had the opportunity to dine at each other's restaurants, but we would introduce ourselves at the bar, buy each other drinks and talk shit. This was how I gathered my intel on who was dining where and what they did and didn't like, and used that knowledge to my advantage as the host. Even when we're not serving you, we are talking about you.

Gin and tonics whizzed past my head. Beers were cracked and spilled on the way to their new owners. The bartender looked at me apologetically, said, 'We're on,' and dimmed the lights.

The room started to heave. I went from being the only person in a cavernous bar to feeling like I was in nightclub. The floors felt stickier, I could see condensation building up in the corners of the wall and could feel damp bodies pressing up against me from all directions.

'What are you doing here, Ho?' It was Baby Chef from work, the only person younger than me in The Restaurant at the time.

'I didn't know what to do on my night off.'

'I would have slept.'

I raised my eyebrow at him.

'Nah, you're right. I would have gotten shitfaced, too.'

'How was tonight?' I needed intel. Even though I hated it, I was lost without my security blanket.

'Yeah, same old. Night Host is good.'

'That's great. Is she coming for a drink?'

'I think so. She's not far behind. I think they're all on their way. I'm going to find a table. Sit with us.' I picked up my drink and nudged my way past sweaty shoulders and elbows towards the back of the room.

'Heeeeey!' The rest of the crew beat Baby Chef and had taken claim over the last table in the room.

'Couldn't stay away,' said Shiteater, one of the senior chefs. Shiteater was given his nickname because one night he was so drunk, he fell on his face and ate shit so hard that he had a scab the size of my palm on his head for a fortnight.

'Nope. I've been here all night.'

'You need to get some friends.' Shiteater was right.

My gin turned into a negroni, then a beer, a few shots and then a whisky before I stumbled home and fell asleep in my shoes. I woke up feeling like a bird shat in my mouth and someone poured sand into my eye sockets. I hated myself for being unproductive. Despite gaining six hours of freedom that night, I hadn't read anything longer than a menu and had written zero words. I had no idea what I even wanted to write, but even practising enough to get writing-fit the way I was piss-fit seemed like an unachieveable goal. My notes from uni were open on the couch and I realised I had to start small. Writing exercises. Describing scenes and evoking emotion without being contrived or sentimental were skills I'd traded in for the ability to carry ten wine glasses at the same time.

I fell asleep later than usual and woke up the most dishevelled I had been since The Restaurant opened. I had a cold shower to wake myself up and deal with the puffiness in my face, and stood under the shower head swallowing large gulps of water until I felt clean.

It was the first morning training session I'd missed in months. I rationalised that I deserved the rest day. I made myself a dry piece of toast and attempted to choke it down while drinking a concoction of Berocca and Hydraltye to lubricate the antacid I was trying to crunch through before dropping a couple of pain killers. I told myself it was the breakfast of champions, then realised I hadn't charged my phone while I was asleep. What a champion.

As I dressed myself for work, I was thankful that I had no hair to style and was too lazy to wear make-up. I moisturised my dull and dehydrated face twice before lathering on sunscreen. I had to admit, if there was ever a day to paint a face onto my face, this was it. The usual eight-minute walk to work felt like a hike as I waited for the painkillers to take effect, and I hoped that this would be the hardest part of my morning. I managed to unlock the front door and disarm the alarm before setting myself up at the end of the bar. While I searched for the will to put together a twenty-four-hour report, Baby Chef walked in to start prep.

'You look like shit.'

'I feel like shit.'

'We did so many shots last night.' I dry-heaved at the thought of alcohol, and remembered all the colours I drank.

I spent the next few hours tucked behind the computer, chugging water until it was time for service. Once people started rolling in and I was on my feet, I realised I was caught in a fog of dumb. I moved a little slower than usual, but I was fine. Night Host arrived for handover with genuine enthusiasm. She'd left at the same time as I had the night before but she was fine. She was more than fine. She was radiant. By comparison, I looked like a steaming pile of dog shit.

As soon as I could leave, I went straight to a Cantonese chop shop for a bowl of curried beef brisket noodle soup with extra tendon and a plate of greens. The vegetables tasted of the bicarb soda the kitchen used to prevent them going brown, but I forced them down because I needed the illusion of health. I was still seedy, but I was restored. I was ready to go home, relax and attempt to use my brain. I thought about the dozens of books on the shelf I'd told myself I'd read once I was given a night off. Being surrounded by neglected words was a depressing reflection of my childhood dreams.

I paid up and stepped onto Little Bourke Street.

'OI, HO!' It was The Greek. 'I'm going to get a few drinks with the guys. Wanna come? I haven't seen you in weeks!'

I was powerless to The Greek. He worked in an Italian

restaurant that took staff meals so seriously they catered to their staff members' likes and dislikes. When the owner heard about our troughs of wings, he instructed The Greek to walk containers of their leftover staff meals to us if they had the time. The Greek had that certain quality to him that made him the perfect bartender: the gift of the gab. A lot of people think they have it, but they just like the sound of their own voice. The Greek had a way of massaging customers to spend way more money than they intended and leave an exceptional tip. He was also a little shit and had memorised the order of the speed rack (the drinks rail that holds all the first-pour alcohols) of most venues from the customer side and was constantly pouring himself drinks in bars he did not man.

When he said, 'the guys' he meant Nugget, the other miscreant from his bar who always had the same night off as him. Nugget was a Kiwi who greeted everyone who walked into the restaurant with an exaggerated 'Ciao', proudly fluent in a language he called 'Choice Bro Italiano'. 'The guys' also meant The Greek's girlfriend, who I was yet to meet.

'I'm fucked from last night. I don't know if I can do it.'

'We are literally fifty metres from the bar. Nugget and Helen are already there waiting for me. It would be a nice surprise if you turned up. C'mon. One drink. Just one.' This was probably how he upsold oysters, pricey Moreton Bay bugs, bottles of Barolo and digestifs to people who'd only intended to stop in for a quick plate of pasta.

'One. And then I am going home.'

We walked into the bar and Nugget stood up, cheering in surprise. He ordered us our first round of drinks. Pure alcohol over ice. I couldn't leave without reciprocating, but Helen beat me to it by buying a round of margaritas. Then we had shots from the bartenders. I don't remember much else of what happened that night, but I know that my arm no longer felt like flesh and bone. It was pure rubber.

My bank statement looked like a list of indignities with the same handful of venues deducting money multiple times a night in sixty-dollar increments. It shadowed my phone bill, electricity and rent. Even with regular free shots and the ten per cent hospitality worker discount that many venues offered, I'd somehow hammered my account so hard that a stop was put on my card and the bank called to check up on suspicious activity.

That should have been enough to prevent me from going out every night, but instead, I just stopped depositing my tips into my account and lived off the cash. It was a classic hospo move. I used to look down on it for being reckless and irresponsible. When I'd moved out of home as a teenager I'd known I couldn't afford to fuck up. I didn't receive any financial assistance, so I put pressure on myself to pay all my bills on time, give myself a budget, and have actual savings and cash to spare in case I was unable to work. I didn't even own a credit card because I didn't trust myself. But I was now two different people. Jess was the smiling face, the host, the fingers behind the consumer-facing accounts of the business – the responsible one. Ho was the animal with an insatiable thirst for anything over forty proof, who would recklessly walk home alone at three in the morning. Jess was the person that everyone saw, but for better or worse, Ho was in charge.

I'd been living in a state of constantly managing hangovers for months when my friend Junior came in for a late lunch one midweek afternoon. It was his night off from working in a fine-dining, farm-to-table, buzzword, media-darling restaurant in the country. For the most part, he loved working and living in the country, but he'd make an effort to come into the city whenever he got sick of eating at his local pubs. These pubs were usually set up for tourists, so they were packed full of booze from the region that he'd tasted thousands of times, and the most exciting thing on the menu was chicken ballotine.

He'd texted me the weekend prior, telling me to keep a seat at the bar for him and my evening free to get loose on his big night in the city. He'd saved up enough tips for his insanely expensive taxi ride home, so I wasn't allowed to back out. 'Fine,' I said. 'Your funeral.'

It also happened to be the day I would be working an hour longer than usual because Night Host had an exam that afternoon. No biggie on my part, but it meant that while he was waiting for me, Junior was treated to the only brand of generous hospitality the bartenders had at their disposal: shots.

Junior was studying for his Wine and Spirits Education Trust (WSET) level three exam, an internationally standardised wine education program that can help you secure your position and pay bracket on a wine team – or, if you're ambitious enough, help you get a job overseas. So he had a voracious hunger for all things old, new and inaccessible to him in country-town bars. Sure, he had the privilege of sitting in on tastings with distributors who were bringing around new drops to sell to all their accounts, but it was a very small sample of what the booze industry had to offer. Junior had not yet tasted the cool, divisive, medicinal and challenging elixir that hospitality workers used as a measuring stick to see if you were the real deal: Fernet-Branca. This drink was known as the Bartender's Handshake. It was a marker of resilience, a palate tester, an energiser, a salve, a way for bartenders to say, 'You're one of us,' while putting hairs on your chest.

Evan looked at me from across the room and I could see that twinkle in his eye that said he was going to either revive or destroy Junior. As a single diner, Junior had already knocked back five snacks, three main dishes, two desserts, a bottle of wine and a cocktail. It's all standard practice for a restaurant worker – you make up for all the calories you missed during the week by eating like it's your death-row meal on your day off. Your body isn't used to digesting it all, so you always require a helper. This is where

Fernet-Branca comes in. Magazines will tell you that it is made of twenty-seven herbs and other ingredients, that it has a higher proof and lower sugar content than other digestifs and is aged in barrels for a year. That's romantic marketing jargon. All you really need to know is that it tastes like a combination of black liquorice and toothpaste. People either love it or hate it, and we were about to find out which camp Junior fell into.

Evan poured out a shot, looked intensely at Junior's face and waited. I could only see the back of Junior's head, but I could tell from his body language that he gritted his teeth in shock. Evan looked at me, smiled and poured another while chanting, 'One of us! One of us!'

By the time I clocked off, Junior had sucked down over half a bottle.

'Are you okay?'

'I feel great! I could eat again!'

'Well, good, 'cause I need to eat. Did you book somewhere for dinner?'

'Yeah, it's around the corner.'

'What time?'

'We've got a few hours.'

Evan handed him the bill and said, 'Fernet's on us, by the way. It was bonus stock.'

Junior over-tipped.

To kill time before dinner, Junior requested that we go to 'that dank bar' I always went to after work. It was the same dank bar I'd spent last Christmas in, the night when everyone told me their secrets.

Junior and I walked the few blocks through the city and arrived at my second home. The bar never felt like it existed in the daytime, even if all the lights were on. Phones only had reception if you were seated next to the street because it was in a basement, and only a select few people knew to find me there if they couldn't get in touch with me.

'Hey, Ho!' Michael knew exactly who he was getting at this hour. He'd taken enough of my money to know that Jess had clocked off for the day. Seeing Michael had become a daily ritual before my post-work shower, as the cocktail bar was right at the middle point between work and home. He always saw me in my post-shift comedown, when I was finally away from the hundreds of chattering voices and desperate to drown all independent thought.

'Hey! This is my friend Junior. Junior, Michael.'

'Nice to meet you.'

'Drinks?' I looked at Junior to take the lead.

'Martinis. Gin. Something interesting. Garnish it in the way you think is best.'

'I like it. You guys gonna hang up at the bar or are you going to take a seat?' I looked around the empty room. Sitting would kill my vibe.

'I think I need to sit down,' said Junior.

'Anywhere you like. I'll bring it over.' My favourite words of consolation. Junior chose a seat by the wall and put his phone out on the table.

'Expecting to hear from someone?'

'Oh, I told a few people I was in town. I don't want to miss them if they text me.' He glanced down at his phone. Michael dropped the martinis and sat down.

'Hey, you guys want to do a shot?'

'Sure!' Junior was on a mission.

Michael came back with three shot glasses in hand. A round of Bartender's Handshakes. The distributor regularly gave out a bunch of bonus stock to all the venues that had been ordering cases of the stuff, which I'm convinced is why so many hospo people were always on the Fernet-Branca train. It's very clever marketing. If a bar was smart, they might include it in their stock count to drive down their average cost of goods. However, having happy staff who will stick around because you treat them like humans, and a bottle up your sleeve to pour to regulars, is smarter than a number on a spreadsheet. We cheered, tapped the bases of the shot glasses on the table, looked each other in the eye and threw the friendly gesture down into our mouths.

'Um ...' Junior picked up his phone in a hurry. 'I think ...' He started typing on his phone. 'I gotta go.'

'Are you okay?'

'I'm so sorry. I think I've had too much to drink. I have to go. I've just booked a cab.' He sat in his chair as though bracing himself, using every little bit of willpower to stay silent and keep everything he'd ingested inside his body. The walk from The Restaurant to the bar had made the booze hit him all at once, and the shot on top did him no favours. I knew that feeling. I felt it every night, except I didn't have food waiting to burst out of my mouth in chunks, just shot upon shot of alcohol sloshing around my empty stomanch inside my fifty-kilogram frame. I was always just hoping to make it home before I lost control.

'Do you want me to cancel the dinner reservation?' Junior kept looking straight ahead and just nodded. He opened his email to give me the details of the restaurant. I picked up my phone, dialled the number, made some reasonable excuse to cover up for the fact that someone in hospitality couldn't hold his liquor, they sent their well wishes and I hung up. Junior skipped the hug, pointed at his phone to gesture that he would text me and ran out. I was secretly relieved because while I couldn't stand being alone with my thoughts, I also didn't want to spend time talking about what I had been up to (nothing) or my feelings (lonely).

I was left alone in the late afternoon with two martinis in a dark basement, so I did what any responsible hospo person would do and drank them both before they even came up to temperature.

By mid-morning, I received a text from Junior apologising for going too hard too early. He blessed me with the story of him having to beg his driver to pull over on the freeway so he could vomit warm, brown chunks all over the side of the road. This was at the beginning of the trip, so there was an hour of him marinating in his own fumes in the back seat while the driver lectured him on the dangers of alcoholism. Junior also used all the wine-tasting verbiage he'd acquired through his WSET education to describe to me how Fernet-Branca tasted warmed up to a moderate thirty-six degrees after being introduced to stomach acid. I told him the moral of the story was that he couldn't drink Fernet-Branca like wine and expect to be okay.

When I went to see Michael on my way home from work, he told me I should eat dinner before having a drink. In the politest way possible, he said I looked wiped and washed out. I insisted that I was fine. I was still training every morning, my quality of work hadn't slipped and no one had posted a negative comment about my behaviour on those crowd-sourced review sites. He wasn't impressed.

'I look pale because I haven't seen the sun in a while.'

'You do know your natural complexion is olive, right?'

'No, I'm naturally jaundice.'

'Don't do that.' I had no idea what he was talking about. 'You always make a joke when someone tries to talk to you about you.'

'But I'm fine.'

'Jess, I say this because we are friends. You are not fine. You are here more than I am, and I work here full-time. I never see you eat dinner and I know you don't eat at work. Yesterday, you drank your drink and your friend's drink and continued to drink until we closed. You fell asleep on the couch when the bar was still full. We took turns telling people to leave you alone, I put a blanket on you, counted the till next to you and walked you home 'cause I didn't want you to get raped or die on the way. Do you even remember that?'

I didn't. I woke up in my own bed the same way I'd been waking up for months, so there was nothing to retrace. My keys were where I had left them, my phone was charged, my wallet was intact, my training gear was all laid out and my bag was packed. I was fine.

'And, Jess,' he continued, 'I wouldn't be bringing this up if it was the first time.'

6

I wasn't in hospital; therefore, I was fine.

I'd been taught that unless it was worth going to hospital for, it wasn't a problem. If I hadn't ended up in hospital yet, the situation could be easily managed. This was probably the result of a neglectful upbringing. If I was in pain or sick, my parents would tell me there was nothing wrong and I was just looking for attention. Under their care, stomach viruses, throat infections, dehydration, allergic reactions and sadness had gone unchecked to the point of hospitalisation. I was taught never to make a fuss or ask for help, and even though the many visits to the hospital should have taught me otherwise, I continued on this way into my adult life. I grew up not understanding when my body was telling me something was wrong, to the point where what was wrong felt normal.

Back in high school, I wound up juggling an in-house school counsellor and a psychologist as an outpatient at the Austin Hospital, because despite receiving perfect marks, I was visibly unhappy, antisocial, had no appetite and had massive issues with authority. On the first week of introductory school camp, I refused to do any of the lame bonding activities and made the science teacher cry. That wasn't the reason the school made me talk to a counsellor, though. The final straw was when I made a disparaging comparison between covalent and ionic bonding and the same science teacher's desperate personal life. I don't remember the details, but I made her cry again.

I was a cunt kid. I also didn't appreciate being told I had to make friends due to coincidence and proximity. I went to a selective state school, so the assumption that we were all smart and could be friends was too simplistic for me. My experience with other children up until this point had been having them call me a chink, ching chong or slope, tell me to go back to where I came from (which was Preston, if you checked my birth certificate), throw rocks at me, or dislike me for being 'weird' because I wasn't a dumbarse. I trusted no one.

I made the involuntary transition from outpatient to inpatient during the summer holidays between year nine and ten. I'd spent year nine applying for a scholarship to study in Germany and got it. My mother hated this and thought the Chinese Christian Baptist Church community would gossip about her, so instead of supporting my decision to further my education in a foreign language, even though it would be at no cost to her (a very important condition for an Asian family), she decided to report to them that I was a risk to myself. Since I was a minor, this triggered a series of events that culminated in me walking out of what was meant to be a discharge appointment, after being told I would have to be admitted into their facility immediately. After that, I was chased down the freeway by a white van and had two fat, male nurses tell me, 'We can either do this the easy way, or we can do this the hard way,' as if they were bounty hunters in some shitty movie. I took one look at their wide loads, made an assumption about their cardiovascular fitness, applied it to the force times mass equals acceleration equation and ran. What I didn't calculate was that one nurse would get in the van, drive and cut me off before the other nurse held me down, stuck me with a sedative and strapped me to a gurney. Back then, I thought people would get out of their cars and help a teenage girl being chased down the freeway by two men in a white van, but no. This moment taught me exactly what to expect from people in society and so far, no one has proven me wrong.

My flight to Germany was meant to be at ten the next morning.

I spent the next few weeks convincing the nurses, psychiatrists and psychologists that my mother was just doing what she always did – posing as a concerned parent to try and control me for her own image. I tried to explain to them that, culturally, spite was a core pillar of being Chinese. It's why we were all so thin despite eating so much rice. Even if I occasionally had suicidal thoughts, believed that existence was futile and resented waking up every morning, I was too spiteful to commit suicide. That was what people expected of me. I was going to make everyone around me suffer by hanging on and doing better at life than them. I was adamant that I was going to outlive everyone else, and my death would be very drawn out, uneventful and natural. It would infuriate everyone. I didn't realise how difficult it would be to explain to middle-aged white men with clipboards that playing the long game is also an inherently Chinese trait, despite pointing at China's one-hundred-year political plan as evidence. It wasn't until they saw my mother bring a bunch of her church friends to sit in the canteen to pray the devil out of me, despite my very loudly expressed opinions on religion and spirituality, that the nurses suspected something. The only time I smiled while I was an inpatient at the hospital was when one of the nurses told them, 'You can pray, but you can't do it here.'

When both my parents finally agreed to a family session, my mother raved at the psychiatrist for the full hour without taking a breath. While my mother held court, I paid all my attention to the psychiatrist and his consistently blank expression. I only saw him take one note that day, and he wasn't even discreet about it. It was: 'Mother is hostile.'

I spent weeks trapped as a 'high dependency' patient, which meant I wasn't allowed out of arm's reach of a nurse at any time, and they revoked me of my shoelaces, pens and my basic human rights while forcing me to take antidepressants and sleeping tablets. They watched me sleep, shit, shower and eat until they finally diagnosed me with dysthymia and officially documented the abusive relationship I had with my mother. The only time I had privacy was when I sat in the closet with the door closed. I was technically an arm's length away from a nurse, but at least I couldn't see that I was being watched.

My experience as an inpatient gave me a proper glimpse into the system, and I saw that it was massively broken. The system was never designed to help people like me. I spent weeks being gaslit by professionals who told me I was being irrational, dramatic and duplicitous until they finally saw my home life in a monitored environment. Up until that moment, they told me I had chosen to be a sad, anxious, paranoid, untrusting insomniac. After spending an hour with my mother and diagnosing me, they pitied me, which felt worse.

I didn't know what to expect from being an inpatient, but the patients were massively outnumbered by the staff. Summer holidays were usually off-season in the underage nut house, so there were only two other patients in the ward when I was there: Bec, who was transferred to the Austin from Shepparton because she burned down part of her family home in a fit of rage, and Sean, who'd chased his mum around the house with an axe. I liked them. We weren't shy about the reasons we were there because we all sat in group sessions together and had to share. The three of us tested the boundaries when we first arrived, which bonded us without words. At first, we all decided to stay in our rooms and not attend group sessions until we were all dragged out. We unsuccessfully agreed to all stop eating, but Sean broke before the day ended. And then we tried sitting in group sessions in silence, but if no one said anything, the session wouldn't end because we had nowhere to be. When we finally gave up on rebelling because it was extending our time in hospital, we all started oversharing. I was forced to distinguish for an all-male, all-white team the difference between how Asian kids are normally beaten, emotionally abused and neglected, and how I was. Bec and Sean understood. The thing we all had in common was an underlying, simmering rage that we mostly turned inwards. We were all also constantly getting the shit kicked out of us by our parents and lived in long sleeves and pants despite it being summer. It took me a while to make the connection that my nose had stopped bleeding every day because my mother wasn't able to use me as a punching bag.

When I was finally discharged as an outpatient, I re-enrolled in school and started making plans to move out. While being an inpatient was intolerable, it was easier to take than living at home. I accepted the fact that I wasn't going to put sixteen thousand kilometres between me and a toxic environment, but a few kilometres would do.

Even though my stay at the Austin was because of my mother, she also resented me for it. Mental illness doesn't exist in Asian culture, so having something documented was an insult to her. It was more gossip fodder among her nosy church friends and the local Cantonese community, even though it had been her decision to bring them to the hospital. To her, I wasn't dysthymic, I just didn't believe in God. And while she denied that I had any form of depression at all, she would swallow my antidepressants and scream at me, claiming I was making *her* depressed. I should not have been surpised. This was coming from the woman who told me that if I quit the piano at ten years old, I would become a prostitute.

When I came home from school after another day of everyone asking me why I wasn't in Germany, and after being called to the counsellor's office for another 'check-in', I found a letter waiting for me on the desk in my room. It was three pages of Times New Roman font, with one-point-five spacing that outlined how my mother considered me her property, which was why she was allowed to physically abuse me. It said that I was making her look bad and that I was going to hell, while she would enjoy all the heavenly riches when she died because her sinful actions would be forgiven. My mother had taken the effort to type this letter up at work, date it, print it off, sign it and stuff it in an envelope as if it were a formal business letter. It made absolutely no sense to me that I was the one who'd spent a few weeks in a psych ward.

Instead of reacting to it, which was exactly what she wanted, I focused on the fact that she'd put her signature on it. This letter was exactly what I needed to leave the family home. I went into my sister's room and asked her if she thought it was enough. She admitted to me that she had already snuck into my room and read it, and was furious with my mother. I didn't understand what she was so angry about because when I was in hospital, she didn't come to see me at all. She was the first-born, and in my eyes, treated like a princess, so I thought she was comfortable being cold and selfish. As an adult, I learned that she was dealing with her own mental health from witnessing everything I'd gone through but not being able to make things better for me. She'd constantly battle my dad behind my back, questioning why he never did anything to help me, but he also didn't know what to do. He was stuck between a daughter and a wife. He couldn't choose. My sister did as sisters do, and showed the letter to my dad, who was heartbroken by it.

I finally had the evidence I needed that my mother was abusing me and that she hated me, but it didn't feel like a win. She wasn't going to change. All that I could change was how much power I could give her to affect me. I kept the letter in my locker at school while I made photocopies and filled out forms from Services Victoria to outline why I was at risk if I stayed at home. With a statement from my high school outlining their concerns for my safety, the letter, and evidence from my stay at the Austin Hospital, I was declared Unreasonable to Live at Home. I was officially my own parent.

I subletted a cheap flat in Blackburn that was close to a train line so I could get to school. Physically, looking after myself wasn't hard. Studying, working, saving money, paying bills, feeding myself and getting from one place to another were things I'd already been doing. But as a sixteen-year-old, sitting alone with my feelings in an empty house was hard. Home had never been a safe space, so I jumped at every creak or shadow in the unit. I also finally had to admit to myself that I had a chemical imbalance and would always feel like this, and I wasn't going to magically feel better by changing my environment. I didn't trust doctors after my stint in hospital, so it became increasingly difficult not to fall into repetitive cycles of depression. I was also managing the pressure to earn money while going to school full-time because Youth Allowance wasn't even enough to cover my groceries. I had no support network and I couldn't afford one either.

School forced me to see a school counsellor and psychologist every week, which chewed up a lot of my time. I mostly sat in silence during these sessions because I physically couldn't talk about the situation I had left. I wasn't ready to acknowledge what I had been through because processing it would render me useless and I wouldn't be able to work. When the counsellor finally got sick of the silence and started asking me questions, I would deflect with jokes or sarcasm. In one session he inappropriately said I reminded him of his young, Asian wife and I never went back. I hardened my heart and stayed busy so I wouldn't have the time to make myself a victim.

I worked casually across retail, data entry and hospitality to support myself through my final years of high school. While data entry and retail paid infinitely better than hospitality and gave me better hours, I gelled more with hospitality people. No one's pasts were used against them, being book smart was irrelevant, everyone was unapologetically themselves without the threat of HR being involved and there was easy access to all forms of mind-altering substances. If I wanted to forget myself, stay awake, go to sleep immediately, experience near-immediate euphoria or live in a semi-permanent haze, someone always knew someone with something.

This was my normal. It had been normal through high school, uni, the pub, all those jobs in between and my year or so at The Restaurant. So, it surprised me that Michael, a facilitator of mind-altering substances, sat me down and spoke to me like a concerned parent (I assumed). After he sent me on my way, dry, but forcibly fed, I admitted to myself that maybe I was a little sad. But I wasn't hospital sad. I wasn't nurse-watching-me-poop-rock-bottom sad. I was definitely not talk-about-my-feelings sad. I wasn't shop-around-for-a-psychologist sad. I was just recognise-that-this-could-be-another-cycle-of-double-depression sad. The one thing I'd learned since my diagnosis was that things could always get worse. Dysthymia means my resting state is pretty much being depressed. But that isn't all. I can get major clinical depression on top of it. Just like having an injury, I'm prone to it. My psyche has the muscle memory of bending the wrong way, I just have to be self-aware enough to make sure it doesn't snap.

So far, I had done everything wrong to deal with a cycle of double depression. I was working too much and drinking every day. I avoided expressing myself and had no support network. I wasn't eating, had been ignoring my interests, like writing and Muay Thai, and had refused to take medication. Some of this was starting to change. My work hours had already been shaved down. I just had to figure out how to drink less. But I'm an all or nothing person. I had to not drink at all. In theory, this is an easy solution – stop drinking – but it made me physically crave sugar. As soon as I walked into The Restaurant, I'd dive into the drawers in the waiters' stations and finish off unwrapped lollies that were left rolling around from the night before. Even though I knew dozens of dirty hands had been in contact with the loose lollies, I ate them out of desperation. I'd put worse things in my mouth. I'd live.

The hurdle of saying no to a free knock-off at work wasn't one I had to jump over. Generally, venues offer staff a beer or a glass of wine after a shift as a thank you for all the shit they've had to endure that day, but at The Restaurant it was against company policy. It was also the reason why a lot of staff didn't stick around; they thought it was dehumanising. I didn't care. The last thing I wanted to do after finishing work was stick around for free.

I made my life for the next few months excruciatingly boring because I forced myself to be responsible. I consistently woke up before my alarm because my quality of sleep improved. I became sharper and stronger in Muay Thai, not because I put in the work, but because I wasn't poisoning myself incrementally hours before turning up to class. Work bothered me less. I was able to tune out the shitty music that pumped through The Restaurant from open to close. Entitled customers had no effect on me because, like with my mother, I stopped giving them power. It was when I was home without distraction that I felt like a sad teenager again. And though it wasn't as dire as being trapped in the suburbs, it wouldn't have made a difference because my brain wouldn't stop. I still couldn't concentrate long enough to read a book, so I leaned into my nerdiness, got myself a VPN and gave myself access to Netflix before it was even available in Australia. I made myself dinner every night, watched an embarrassing amount of trash television and got fat. Not the kind of fat my confirmed bachelor line manager might point out, but the kind of fat that my Asian family would make a fuss about.

There are only two acceptable body shapes for Asians: skinny-fat and fat. Skinny-fat is the untoned size zero that Chinese people consider 'hot', and being fat means you're rich because you can afford to eat that much and not give a shit. I was too fat to be skinny-fat and not fat enough to be rich-fat. I was also not rich, so I couldn't let myself get fat. What was worse, I was putting on muscle. In Asian circles, that meant I was too masculine for my sex. I hadn't spoken to my parents in years, but I could still hear my mother's voice telling me that I wasn't allowed to eat dinner. Now, I shut her up by shoving food in my mouth and working on my glamour muscles. *I am health*, I told myself, deeply aware that my mental health was a dumpster fire. If I were a cartoon villain, this would be my origin story.

'I'm having dinner with a friend,' 'I'm babysitting my sister's kids,' and 'I've just paid rent,' were high-rotation excuses for not going out with people from work when we finished a shift at the same time. Even if the invitation was to share a plate of dumplings in Chinatown, I knew that I would end up pouring wine into every hole in my face.

A normal person would probably have converted to a wholesome human in this time away from late-night city life. I ended up like that quiet kid in high school who didn't talk much but had the capacity to become a serial killer. I did kill chickens as a child, so it tracks.

Books were still a challenge for me. I'd get a few paragraphs in and realise I hadn't paid attention to anything I'd read. So I started small. I read reviews of restaurants, but I'd lose interest halfway through any description of décor. I couldn't look at Twitter because it felt like work and I was starting to get sick of it. I avoided Facebook at all costs because people I hadn't spoken to for years were trying to kiss my arse so I would get them a table at The Restaurant. Poetry was not for me; it was all full of subtlety and feelings and I didn't want to be in touch with mine. I wanted to stamp them out. And then I discovered Reddit.

Reddit was perfect for my hyperactive mind and superficial interests because it was an aggregate of all the most horrible, immature, ridiculous and outrageous stuff on the internet. There was also a lot of educational content, but when a resource is used for evil, it is much more entertaining. It also appealed to my love of lurking. I didn't have to contribute. I had front-row seats to petty arguments, embarrassing stories and people losing their minds over conspiracy theories. By day, I was a fully functioning member of society in a relatively social job. By night, I became a reclusive internet voyeur, sitting in the dark, hunched over a coffee table howling at the misfortune of strangers.

I knew I had to stop when I spent a whole night reading an Ask Me Anything thread from a vacuum repair technician. I was instantly obsessed by the random shit he found inside machines (lots of bullets, reptile eggs and dead infant mice), and then I became incensed by how much he hated Dysons after I'd just laid down more money for one than I had paid for all my whitegoods put together. After I'd been laughing at the internet all this time, the internet was now laughing at me.

All the blue light from the computer screen didn't help my pallid complexion. I was now working a luxurious forty-hour week in an industry where the bare minimum was sixty. Everyone assumed I had been blowing them off to party and was oddly, deceptively functional during the day. People made an effort to ask me out for breakfast on the weekends, even if it meant they lost precious hours of sleep before work. There were a few 'Are you okays' mixed with thinly veiled suggestions to go to a gallery or watch a movie. I denied every offer of dinner, which made people even more suspicious because of my girth. It got to the point where I stopped hanging out with people from work altogether because they'd either want to drink or talk about feelings, or were higher than me on the organisational chart.

My sad-person spiral should have seen me drowning in trite drug and booze-fuelled orgies, the way most hospo people crashed and burned, but mine was just self-imposed isolation with an internet connection. How Asian of me.

I received an email from Our Fearless Leader. He never wasted my time with long-winded messages. It just said, 'Let's schedule a one-on-one meeting this week. Not Friday.'

My mind started backtracking through everything at work. I was never late, so that couldn't be it. My reports were always sent off on time. I checked the addresses of everyone who received reports, I didn't fuck up and send it to anyone external. I went through all the blogs, social media accounts and major broadsheets and found nothing negative that needed to be addressed. There were no changes to the roster, so I didn't need to cover for anyone. Even if I did, that request would come via text. There were no major disputes between the front and the back of the house that

I had any intel on. Management never gave a shit about everyone boning each other unless it involved a member of management, so it wasn't that. No senior member of staff had recently quit or was fired, so they couldn't be asking me to post a job ad. Then I thought back on everything I had said to any staff member at work. Of course I was crass and brash, but so was everyone else. If I got a warning about the way I spoke to people at work, so would everyone else. Maybe they thought my role was of no use to them anymore? Maybe they needed more money for the new venue they were developing and they were going to take it from my salary? If I was going to be made redundant, this was the time. I'd saved up so much money from not going out that I had a cushion to get me through until I found a new job. Plus, there was all the holiday pay I hadn't used.

I told myself to stop freaking out. I would be fine. I also had no pride or shame. I would stack shelves if I had to. If I was going to be let go, I'd work as much as I could before that. I responded to Our Fearless Leader with, 'How's Thursday after lunch?'

The threat of losing my job was in the back of my mind for the entire shift. I worked alongside Senior Manager the next day and he either had the best poker face I had ever seen, or had no idea I was getting tossed. I spoke to Night Host during handover and she had no intention of working more, so she wasn't absorbing my shifts. We had a management meeting and Our Fearless Leader smiled at me the way he always did, nodded along to my reporting, laughed at my jokes and said goodbye like we were old friends when it was all over. What a two-faced motherfucker.

As I was leaving the meeting room, he doubled back and said, 'Oh, sorry, Jess. I forgot to respond to your email. Thursday after lunch is fine. I'll pop in before your shift is over.' He pranced off into the distance and I thought to myself, *What's wrong with now? Rip the Band-Aid off already!* I worked the entire lunch service in a rage. If I was going to be fired, it better be for a reason. One of the chefs asked me if I had my period because I was so narky. I responded with, 'But how can you tell when I'm always a cunt?'

Thursday finally arrived and I talked myself down from committing arson as a pre-emptive measure. As expected, Our Fearless Leader 'popped in' a little earlier than usual, today in a new pair of Prada boots he was showing off to everyone, and asked me if it was okay if we talked downstairs.

'Sure.' I noticed he was empty-handed. If he was firing me, there was no physical evidence.

We sat in a booth in the bar and he said, 'So, you've been working here for a while now.'

'Yes.' I should have recorded this conversation for Fair Work.

'I know we haven't spoken about it before, but I was just reviewing everyone's hours, leave and overtime the other day,' here it comes, 'and you have a lot of leave accrued.'

Yes, and that's what I am going to live on until I find a new job.

'I think you need to take a holiday. I've had one. Senior

Manager has had one. Executive Chef's gone on two! Plus, you look really tired and everyone keeps asking me if you're okay.'

'So, you're having a meeting with me to tell me to take leave?'

'I want you to book a holiday within the next week and tell me the dates so I can approve them before I approve anyone else's leave.'

'Oh.'

'When was the last time you had a holiday?'

Never. I'd been working to survive since I left home in high school. I didn't have the luxury of going on holiday. Even when other restaurants I'd worked at were closed over Easter or Christmas, I'd stayed at home and slept the whole way through. Going on holiday seemed like a very privileged thing to do. My parents always told me that holidays were for white people, and I was still drenched in immigrant guilt.

'I think it would be good for you. A change of scenery. Get out of Australia. Go to New York. Get away from your computer and emails. I want you to do nothing for at least three weeks.'

'How much time have I accrued?' I had never not worked for three weeks since the day I started working.

'A lot more than that.'

I went home that afternoon and looked at flights. I had no idea where to go. I had such a long list of places I wanted to visit, and Germany was one of them. But it was still too soon. I wasn't ready for that. Our Fearless Leader had suggested New York, and it was on the list. I checked the exchange rate and, for once, our dollar was worth more than the US dollar, so that was settled. Over the weekend, I booked my tickets and accommodation, exchanged money, sent through my dates and I felt something I hadn't felt in a long time. I wasn't sad, bored, hopeless or anxious. I was excited. Maybe I *could* lift myself out of a cycle of depression by putting sixteen thousand kilometres between me and life. Maybe a few kilometres wasn't enough. It was a decade late, but I would finally test out that theory.

7

Our Fearless Leader may have asked me to take a holiday at the end of spring, but I couldn't leave until the middle of summer. There is an unwritten rule in hospitality that says asking for a holiday during the busiest periods of the year (Christmas, New Year's, Australian Open, Melbourne International Comedy Festival, Grand Prix, Melbourne Fringe Festival, Melbourne Writers Festival, Melbourne International Arts Festival) means you're a delusional arsehole. It's audacious, it's rude and it tells management that you're not a team player. There was the pain of waiting months to physically check out, but I was already mentally vacant. Thankfully, I had time to plan for the fifty-degree temperature drop and culture shock.

I'd made a list of pros and cons in my head when I decided to go to New York. The exchange rate, not having to learn a new language, easy-to-navigate transport system and the rise of Airbnb were all big pros. The cons involved packing heavy, the near twenty-four-hour flight and the imperial system. My plan was to go to New

York and get fat, then come back to Melbourne and melt it all off in the residual summer heat. Genius.

This was a time when the food world was intensely blokey and dictated by the stars of the San Pellegrino Top Fifty awards. Everything was about showmanship, bold flavours, extremes, intense heterosexual masculinity and meat. This was the era before Mario Batali got MeToo-ed out of the industry, when Wylie Dufresne still had a restaurant to serve eggs out of, René Redzepi hadn't gone mental on Instagram over Mexican mangoes yet, Massimo Bottura was on the cusp of gaining mainstream attention, and both Jonathan Gold and Anthony Bourdain were still alive. These were the years when *Lucky Peach* was insanely popular, moving food magazines away from the lifestyle space by presenting the exact opposite of glossy pages, women laughing at salad and quick, healthy weeknight meals (but at least it wasn't blindingly white). American titles were being run like men's magazines, focusing on trends and rapid consumerism. Ethics did not exist. The year was 2013. What a time to be alive.

What a time to be a cis-hetero man working in the food industry.

I was so naively obsessed with these American culinary gods that they did not seem real. They were as untouchable, fictitious, and intimidating to me as Tony Soprano and Don Draper. I asked myself why I hadn't thought about going to America before to experience this incredible, dynamic, cutting-edge food scene. The way I saw it, being at the arse end of the world – so geographically isolated and unable to access the same ingredients from specific producers – in addition to being a recently-colonised country with an undefined cuisine, meant our food scene was backwards, bland and stale.

All the research I did back then is the opposite of what I would do today. I pored over the *Eater* heatmap, read *New Yorker* profiles, interviews and reviews. I watched *Vice's* 'Munchies' channel to see which chefs were partying where. I am ashamed to say that I even paid attention to what *Bon Appétit* told me to do.

The spreadsheet and personalised Google Maps page I created for myself just looked like I'd consciously dropped pins on big-name, penis restaurants. There were only two that were run by women and, unsurprisingly, they were both white. Shame on me. Double shame on me for wanting to eat at so many ramen joints outside of Japan (again, I blame *Lucky Peach*). I didn't know better. I was enamoured by all these testosterone-driven publications, influenced by the Melbourne Food and Wine Festival's international headlining chefs and hardcore hipster bro-palates. I'd hate myself if I didn't think it was punishment enough that I wasted a trip to New York eating below-average bowls of noodles suspended in liquified pork fat.

The last day before I'd clock out for three weeks, Our Fearless Leader asked me to talk to one of the new staff members in the bar. I went through the motions to get through the shift and I had absolutely no heart in what I was doing. At four, an hour before I was meant to leave, I met Mike, a new hire in the bar downstairs who was also finishing his degree at RMIT. Our Fearless Leader had accepted his proposal to use the bar to launch emerging artists in untraditional spaces and wanted me to help him. I told him I was leaving for New York, so I'd come back to him with a strategy. He responded with, 'Yeah, sick.' I forgot about him for a month, but little did I know that this indifferent conversation would upend my entire life.

No one told me that flying economy to New York meant that after the first eight hours, the entire back end of the plane would turn into a tin can of farts and body odour. The taxi driver who picked me up from JFK and deposited me at my Crown Heights Airbnb assured me that I did not in fact have stink lines coming off me, and he'd had worse people in the back of his car. That statement didn't quite assure me, but I felt like it was a very New York thing to say. There is always someone hotter, smarter, richer and stinkier than you. I could live with that.

The Airbnb I chose was a renovated warehouse filled with reclaimed wood, oddities and instruments, and was home to a furniture fabricator, a musician and an artist. The fabricator, Ken, built the place with his bare hands and the home was an installation in itself. There weas a studio, darkroom and workshop on site, and we were free to use them all. They kept three rooms aside for Airbnb guests, which their landlord didn't know about. Another check on the New York experiences list. The introduction to the warehouse included a tour, how to work the taps in the shower that were accidentally installed backwards, a warning about everyone staying up until five every morning, a warning about Ken walking around naked when he showered, and an aviation (a sweet gin cocktail) for everyone around the ten-person dinner table, where we ate to the accompaniment of an acoustic guitar. The musician, Tilly, had just learned how to make them and bought a handle of gin that afternoon, so the house decided it was the drink of the month. Cheers. Another New York experience.

When I arrived at this warehouse Airbnb, my home for the next three weeks, I showered. Twice. I was convinced that, like a piece of meat in herbs and spices, I had marinated in farts and the smell was more than skin deep. Everyone in the house was just waking up, even though it was well past nine, and Tilly was waiting on a couple to arrive for check-in. I was jetlagged, but in reverse. I thought by not sleeping on the plane, I would pass out after getting settled. I decided to put on half the clothes I'd packed and go for a walk for (you guessed it) ramen.

'A blizzard's coming,' said Tilly.

'I'll be all right.'

'We won't send a search party,' said Ken.

I laughed and somehow walked all the way to Park Slope. If you're wondering how the ramen was at the place I went to, the venue no longer exists. I sat at the bar, had a few drinks and watched the endless delivery orders walk out the door. This was also the time before we had Uber Eats in Australia. *You really can get everything delivered in New York*, I thought.

'Nice of you to brave the weather to join us,' said the bartender, eager for tips. 'You're the only person who has dined in tonight.'

'The blizzard's not that bad.' It was cold and I was slipping through sheets of ice and wading through urban snow, but the wind didn't spank me in the face the way a southerly gust from Antarctica does during a Melbourne winter.

'Where are you from?' Oh, this question.

'Oh, my parents are from Hong Kong.'

'That's not what I mean. Your accent. What is it? British?'

'Australia.'

'Oh, that's cool. I've always wanted to go to Australia, but it's so far.'

'Tell me about it. I just got in.'

'What, like this week?'

'As in, like, this evening.'

'Damn. Let me guess, you work in a restaurant.'

'How did you know?'

'You're sitting here, dining on your own, drinking on your own, you're not checking your phone or waiting for a date and only neighbourhood people come here. How did you find us?'

'I think it was *Eater*.'

'Oh yeah, we got so busy after they pumped us up.'

'Can I ask you a question?' I trickled the last drop of whisky into my mouth.

'Sure.' The bartender touched the base of my glass and glanced at it as a way to ask if I wanted another. I nodded.

'How do you tip for drinks here? First time, first restaurant. I don't know the rules outside of dining.'

'Generally, a dollar a drink. A few dollars if you're buying rounds. More if you're flirting with the bartender.' He placed another inch of whisky in front of me.

'Oh, so you normally tip after each drink order?' I pulled out a few singles and placed them on the bar.

'If you're paying per drink. Do you not tip in Australia?'

'Nah, we get paid a "living wage" so tipping isn't that big. Mainly in restaurants, you'll get ten per cent if you're lucky. No one normally tips in bars unless you're hospo. Then you usually leave some change behind.'

'That explains why Australians are such bad tippers.'

'And we're cheap.' A group of guys walked through the door, sat down at the bar next to me and said hi. I could immediately tell they were hospitality workers because they were inappropriately dressed for the weather. When you work in a restaurant, the room is always around twenty-four degrees so that it's comfortable for the guests, which makes it way too hot to work in. The hour after any shift is over is used to cool your body down. None of these guys had jackets on, and I could smell sweat and used oil wafting from the dirty clothes in their bags.

'Guys, this is Jess. Jess is from Australia and works in restaurants too. She just got in.'

'Front or back?'

'Front and office.'

'Cushy.'

'It is now.'

'We're all going to hit up this new bar a few blocks away if you want to come.' Usually, I don't tag along with groups of strange men in a foreign city I've been in for less than five hours, but there is a certain kind of trust between people who work in hospitality. My youth and stupidity told me that if I could rely on someone during service, I could rely on them out of service. I had the blind trust of a child, which could either result in danger or lead me to that magical intersection of excitement and adventure.

After the bartender at the ramen shop cleaned down, we made our way to a new-style sports bar that was light on sport, heavy on dark spirits and served only pork. I heard one of the guys mumble something about how it had some affiliation with one of the contestants who lost on Top Chef but made a really big name for himself. 'I bet it's the first time half of this room has been in Park Slope,' said one of the guys to me, completely missing the irony that it was genuinely my first time in Park Slope. My impression of this bar was that it was extremely American. Alcohol had been fat-washed in bacon-this or rendered-pork-that. Every pour was at least three fingers high, and I had no recollection of how I got back to my Airbnb at the end of the night.

When I woke up, I felt drier than a box of sand. It was the first time in months that I had drunk. I went through the checklist every woman does after a night of being irresponsible: check if you've been penetrated, check that you're alone, check that you have your ID, cards and keys, and find your shoes. My hands smelled like hot sauce, my clothes smelled like cigarettes and wood smoke. At least my wallet wasn't quite as empty as it would have been in Melbourne. Australia's WET tax on alcohol means even before we look at booze, it is forty per cent more expensive than in the rest of the world. I flashed back to eating some ribs at some stage of the night. On my laptop, there was a poorly folded napkin with fifteen venues scrawled on it in semi-legible writing, signed off with, 'Welcome to New York.' They were recommendations from the guys at the restaurant. It was another list of male chefs to give my money to.

I wish I could tell you that my first night in New York didn't break me, but after taking time off from poisoning myself in thirty-millilitre increments, I should not have gone to the country of the free-pour and no WET tax with only soupy pork and solid pork to soak it all up. I spent my afternoon with my head in the toilet, vomiting up bile. *This is the intersection between naivety, excitement and magic,* I thought to myself as I uncontrollably hurled up green, bitter foam.

After I cleaned myself up, I realised everyone else was still asleep. I saw the dirty glasses on the kitchen table and remembered that I didn't go straight to bed when I got back to the Airbnb. I drank cocktails with Tilly, Ken and a bunch of their friends while debating the origins of scallion (I had to use to local dialect – they're not called spring onions in America) oil noodles, before Tilly played the guitar and sang until sunrise. This explained why one gush of vomit was particularly sweet when all I remembered drinking was whisky.

I started doing the dishes and a guy came in through the workshop.

'Hi, I'm Ed. I work for Ken. I'm just coming to use the bathroom.'

'Hey, I'm Jess. I'm staying here for three weeks.'

'Big night last night?'

I started filling the sink with hot water and the sticky cocktail glasses and said, 'How did you guess?'

Ed explained that he'd tried to use the bathroom earlier, but I was throwing up in it. He also said Ken didn't usually sleep through a Friday because it was when they put in orders or delivered pieces to clients.

'I'm going to pick up some food for everyone, do you want some?' Ed asked.

'That sounds great. What are you getting? I can give you some cash.'

'Considering the night you've had, I am going to go to the roti shop. I'm from Trinidad and this place does food that reminds me of home. Do you trust me to order for you?'

'That sounds amazing.'

Ed took the business truck, because while I was sleeping, the blizzard had dumped multiple feet of snow over the city and the streets were blocked. He came back with steaming bags of roti, doubles and curry. I cleaned down the table and he lay out all the food, explaining to me what everything was. 'Buss Up Shut is torn up roti. You break it up while you're cooking it and it mops up stews really nicely.'

'Why is it called Buss Up Shut?'

'Buss Up Shut is a busted-up shirt. The roti looks like a torn up shirt. Doubles are my favourite. They'll keep you full all day. It's channa on fried bread. Eat it with the tamarind sauce. Oh, and I just got some vegetables as well. Eat that with the Buss Up Shut. There are some potato and channa-stuffed rotis as well, but they're two meals in one.'

'This all looks incredible. I haven't come across food like this in Australia. How much do you I owe you?'

'This all only cost thirty dollars. Don't worry about it. I'm sure you'll be buying me lunch while you're here.' We sat in silence tearing through the food. The buttery roti, deep, complex gravies, surprising bursts of heat, feathery soft baras carrying a flood of earthy chickpeas punctuated by a high-acid tamarind jolt brought me back to life. I was sitting in an ice-cold warehouse with an almost-stranger, the two of us steaming our faces with food from his culture. We were eating with our hands. This was the New York experience I'd been looking for, not the bowls of sad soup, fat-washed liquor, celebrity chef bars and displays of ego.

'Thanks so much, Ed. That's the best food I have eaten in ... at least a year.'

'It's my pleasure. I'll show you where the shop is after they plough the streets. I'd stay in today if I were you. I might have to sleep in a spare room here 'cause I won't be able to get home. That's why I bought so much food.'

'So, when do you think everyone's going to wake up?'

'When did you go to bed?'

'About sunrise.'

'No one is going to move until about nine-thirty, ten. It's normal for them.'

'How do they live?'

'They're artists.'

No one showed themselves until 10.30. The first thing Tilly did was make a cup of tea and an aviation.

'Has anyone rung the doorbell?'

'I haven't heard anything.'

'We're getting a new check-in today, but he's being held up from the weather. Flying in from Canada.'

'Oh, cool.'

Tilly rolled a cigarette and used a piece of string she'd found lying on the dining room table to secure her hair off her face. She lit the cigarette and started searching through her phone, ashing into a novelty ashtray that featured one pig fucking another and the words 'Bacon in the makin'. She picked a stray piece of tobacco off her tongue and said to me, 'Oh, he's five minutes away. He's named Clarke. He stays with us quite a bit because he uses the darkroom. He's a photographer who also sometimes teaches English Literature at one of the colleges. I think he's here to photograph for Fashion Week. You'll love him.'

'Look who I found.' Ed brought Clarke in through the workshop. 'Tilly, I bought your favourites from the roti shop. There are heaps in the fridge. Help yourself.'

'My hero! Clarke, this is Jess. She's here for three weeks on holiday. I'm sure you'll spend a bit of time hanging out together.'

'Am I in my usual room?'

'You sure are.' Clarke dumped his things and poured himself a cup of tea. He didn't need an intro, he was already boiling the kettle to refill the pot and helping himself to one of Tilly's cigarettes.

'Where's Ken?'

'Still asleep, probably.'

'No, I'm not.' And just as I had been warned, he was completely naked, not even bothering to cover his sub-zero-temperature-affected junk with his towel, and headed for the shower. His naked dash was more of a slow, proud slink to display his frozen balls, alcohol belly and the tuft of hair on his lower back, and his trip back to his room to get dressed was even slower.

'You'll get used to it,' said Tilly, 'Also, it's Friday night. What are we doing?'

'We can't do anything. We're trapped.'

'The blizzard's stopped, but the streets are filled with snow. My taxi had to follow a snow plough to get here.'

We sat around the dining-room table, drinking and feasting on Trini food when Ken suggested we sled in the snow.

'We don't have a sled,' said Tilly.

'There's a box we're not using.'

In my head I saw Magritte's *This is Not a Pipe*.

This is Not a Sled.

'Are there any hills nearby?' I asked, naively.

Ken smiled at me and said, 'We don't need a hill. We have the truck, some rope, helmets and safety goggles.' The way these people lived amazed me.

'Here we go!' Ed gathered all the materials and came back to the main room. 'I brought some gloves for the rope as well, so you don't burn your hands.'

We all sat in the box to see who would be able to go for a sled. Everyone fit except for Ken because of his ridiculously long legs. As the main Airbnb guest, I was given the honour of going first.

We went out into the streets that were eerily empty, especially for a Friday night in Brooklyn. Everyone loaded up in the trailer facing the back of the truck. Ed nominated himself to hold onto the rope from the truck after he pushed my head into a bicycle helmet, adjusted my safety goggles, handed me the gloves and told me how to communicate with him about the speed of the truck. He said, if I ever felt unsafe, to just to let go. Clarke grabbed his camera to document the whole thing.

I gripped the knotted rope with welding gloves that were too big for my hands, sat in the box and wedged my feet into the corners, then Ken started to drive. We started with ten miles per hour, then twenty. We finally decided thirty miles per hour was the absolute fastest we would go. The wind whipped my cheeks and my sides as I glided on the soft, freshly fallen snow and my lungs filled with ice. Then we started to slow down. We'd come across someone who was trapped in his car, so we dug him out with our bare hands. It was a parent of a newborn who had decided he was going to nap in his car, away from the crying, and he'd stupidly left his phone indoors.

Once he was free we took turns soaring across the ice-slicked streets until we pulled up at the lights next to a plough truck. The driver rolled down his window and told us to turn right because the plough hadn't hit those streets yet. We'd have at least half an hour. *This* was the intersection between naivety, excitement and magic that I'd been looking for. When we got back to the warehouse, we were all dripping from melted snow. We made hot toddys, scrambled a dozen eggs and shoved them into tortillas with a buffet of hot sauces that ranged in Scoville units from warm to the equivalent of giving Satan a rim job. I went to bed at four while everyone stayed up and did more of that bohemian, Moulin Rouge shit they were into.

The next day I ventured out to Manhattan and nearly choked to death by breathing in a spoonful of cumin-laced chilli oil from a plate of hand-pulled noodles at the no-frills, food court-style shop Xi'an Famous Foods. 'No tip as we don't give service,' said a sign at the register. You ordered at the counter, picked up your food when an elderly woman screamed your number out at the dumbwaiter, carried it to your table on a tray, and threw away your own trash. The food was so spectacular, I ate there three more times.

I wandered through galleries in Chelsea and ran into Clarke on his way to shoot a runway show for Fashion Week. He took me along, pretending I was his assistant. I was suddenly surrounded by insanely beautiful, manicured and famous people who were walking advertisements for high-end labels. I stood a few feet from ridiculously cool actors who I later recategorised as jerks when they ignored no-smoking signs and dismissed security guards who were just doing their jobs. We drank free cocktails from hot but terrible bartenders and ended up eating Best Pizza's ricotta, mozzarella, caramelised onion and parsley-topped white slices on the sidewalk on the way back to the warehouse. Clarke considered himself a connoisseur of the New York slice. He said it was the perfect food to eat when your invoices are always paid late and you've always got something in one hand. He considered Best's white slice New York's finest.

Between disappointing bowls of ramen, I hit up cocktail bars. I'd received tips from well-travelled, well-respected food writers and bartenders back home, so they had to be good. What I didn't account for was that everyone would be trying to impress me with their recommendations. I was directed to very shiny hotel bars where I'd be drinking next to Wall Street arseholes, off-duty models and very expensive sex workers. The service was sharp, the drinks were precise, the room was immaculately styled, but it lacked personality. It was all image and no substance. Every time I walked to the bathroom, despite not wearing a uniform, people would try to order a drink off me or ask me where the toilet was. My hospo walk, the walk that said, 'I know where I am going and I am getting there quickly,' was a signifier to regular people that I lived a life of service. It also tipped off any other hospo worker in the room that I was one of them. This is how I ended up in Alphabet City at a dive bar drinking lukewarm beer with a buffet of cold Colombian food. The drinks were cheap, the room was pumping and the food was surprisingly excellent. In case you're wondering, I did not get food poisoning from the trays of starch and meat left out for an unknown amount of time at an ambient temperature in a cramped and steamy bar with a B-grade health rating.

The only recommendation I'd received from a friend in Melbourne that didn't suck was from someone who'd spent six months working in New York, living on a waiter's wage. He directed me to a Korean restaurant by Hooni Kim, who had just opened up a second joint the week I arrived. It was, unsurprisingly, a no-bookings venue. As a solo diner, I didn't have to wait. I was directed to the bar and offered half portions. I ordered a haemul pajeon (seafood pancake), duo of kimchi, the grilled heart and skin from a freshly killed chicken (the venue boasted that the carcases were still warm on delivery), jokbal (five-spice braised trotter) and makgeolli (sparkling rice wine) from tap and soju. Hooni was instructed by our mutual friend to look out for me, and we ended up drinking whisky together towards the end of the night. From ten o'clock, single diners took up the bar seats next to me and were served without even communicating.

'I'll introduce you to my old colleagues,' said Hooni. It turns out that he spent the formative years of his cooking career in the kitchen at Daniel, a restaurant I knew I could never afford to go to, or get a booking at, which was associated with prestige and admired by people both in and out of the industry. Usually, when someone works at a restaurant like Daniel, they make a point to mention it on their website when they go out on their own. Hooni didn't, which said a lot about him as a person, and more about him as a chef.

'I make a twelve-hour broth for a spicy Korean ramyun that I only serve from ten. It's not written on the menu, but it's pretty much made for hospitality workers. Everyone here is getting a bowl.' We all nodded at each other around the bar, raised our frosty makgeolli glasses and took a sip. A procession of golden aluminium ramyun pots came from the kitchen, steaming with a rich broth, slices of pork belly, beansprouts and an egg. Hooni laid some cutlery in front of me and said, 'Don't think you're getting out of it.' Even though it was a deviation from the Japanese-style ramen I had been hunting down, it shat all over the cultural-appropriation noodles I'd been eating so far.

'Hey, I'm doing a video in Flushing about Korean food tomorrow. It's going to be filmed, but we're going to ten restaurants so we need mouths. Do you want to come?'

In less than twenty-four hours, I would be waiting at the station exit at Flushing for Hooni to pick me up in his car. We'd meet the host and cameraman at the first stop – a Korean barbecue restaurant specialising in aged kimchi and pork. The next venue specialised in beef, and the owner wouldn't let any parts of the meat char, slapping Hooni's hands away from the tongs and snipping at the edges of beef with scissors. 'Koreans are very health conscious and think the Maillard reaction causes cancer,' said Hooni, to the camera.

I experienced Korean-Chinese steamed buns, learned of the Chinese influence in jajangmyeon (black bean noodles) and jjamppong (spicy seafood noodle soup), and was educated about the difference between Japanese and Korean sushi.

Hooni pointed towards a tank and the chefs clubbing fish behind the counter. 'Koreans literally beat the fish to death because the body responding in shock and stress makes the flesh sweeter and chewier, whereas Japanese people kill their fish ike-jime-style and age them for a softer mouthfeel.' Even in describing live-action death, Hooni had such a warm demeanour about him. Later that year, he'd be cast as a judge on Korea's MasterChef.

I saw how drunk people get while eating gamjatang (pork bone and potato soup); inhaled my first soondae (Korean blood sausage), which changed my life; had clams explode in my face over a grill at a joomak (pub); and drank litres of Cass beer and soju.

'See how the waiters leave the empty bottles on your table? It's because when Koreans get drunk and we get cut off, we like to argue. Now, the waiter can point at the table and say, 'See how drunk you are! You've had twelve bottles. No more for you!' As if on cue, a woman stumbled into the kitchen and was kicked out by the chef.

'Oh no, she can't find the bathroom,' said Hooni, graciously translating the Korean drama unfolding in front of us. She walked straight out the front door, dropped her pants and pissed in the snow. *Wow, this is the intersection between naivety, excitement and magic.* I beamed.

She came back to her table and continued eating.

That evening I ditched the supposedly well-researched list I'd made back home. Instead, I relied on recommendations from Filipino bartenders, Haitian taxi drivers, Mexican kitchen hands and Chinese grocers. The best meals I ate in New York came from endorsements by people who had been displaced, found their communities and carved out a space for themselves in the city. I was in the busiest, loudest and craziest places in the world, and it was the first time I noticed that my head was quiet. I had clarity. Between urban sledding, self-inflicted stranger danger, celebrity spotting and probable alcohol poisoning, my brain found the truth, and the truth was: popular food culture was fucked and I hated my life because I had made myself part of the problem. I felt relief being in a different country because I could be a different person in America, but as soon as that plane landed in Melbourne, I would be that arsehole censoring parts of someone else's culture and selling the easily digestible bits to a rich, white audience. I was going home to a job where I'd be pushing white faces cooking Thai food and dumbing down an entire cuisine into entertainment. I'd be working in a restaurant that prided itself on 'elevating' and 'reinventing' food that didn't require elevating or reinventing in the first place. In Melbourne, the intersection that I lived in was naivety and stupidity.

I wasn't depressed. I was guilty.

8

I wasn't nearly as fat as I'd hoped to be when I got home. Even though I had been putting on weight before my holiday, it was only because I'd been making myself dinner. Breakfast and lunch were meals that had always escaped me. I'd thought of New York as my opportunity to store nuts for the winter, but I didn't account for shivering and regulating my own body temperature as an effective means to burn calories. It was a blessing in disguise. Melbourne was in the middle of a heatwave. There was a predicted ten days in a row of forty-plus-degree days, and the nights wouldn't fall below thirty-five. I'd just come from a fast city full of fast walkers and fast talkers making fast money, and the blistering heat slowed everything down. Strides were shortened, vowels became stretched and elongated, time slowed down.

I was greeted with a 'Goooooooood to seeeeeeeeee yaaaaaaaaaa baaaaack, luuuuuuuuuuv,' by the building manager. Readjusting to the Australian accent, pace and temperature was more jarring than I'd expected.

'It's called the post-holiday blues,' said Our Fearless Leader. 'Everyone gets it.' And then I saw it. Inside his Prada boots and behind his fake smile was a person who didn't love his job. There was just a person who loved what the job afforded him and gave him access to. He'd reconciled the balance of his life and he was happy to work to live, not live to work.

It was healthy. The benefit of working in a restaurant is that when you walk out the front door, you leave the job behind. If you're smart enough (and not the owner), you don't take the annoying customers, work drama or the numbers home with you. But I was starting to see my guilt everywhere in venues that were copying the 'diluted ethnic cuisine for beginners' business model. They saw the huge success of The Restaurant and were hoping to replicate it. Every neon sign that was being made, every overly cutesy, monosyllabic, nonsensical restaurant name, every announcement that 'our dishes are designed to share' rather than labelling the menu 'banquet-style', every stupid Twitter account created for a restaurant with a millennial voice made the acid in my stomach swell up to my throat.

I should have known. My parents didn't teach me much, but they taught me how to eat. The number-one rule of going to a restaurant serving ethnic food is that the majority of people eating in the restaurant have to be from the cuisine's cultural background. I looked around The Restaurant. While I knew it was a white restaurant because of the white owner, the people who dined here would call it Thai. They'd also use the wrong cutlery to shovel Southeast Asian herbs and spices into their mouths while making an excellent reproduction of a nineties Tommy Hilfiger ad.

I made a point to say hi to my colleagues on my first day back rather than diving into my laptop and grunting acknowledgements to people as they clocked on. Ev was sick of the night crew packing down the bar 'like clowns'. He was exhausted, fed up and had run out of spherical ice with a flower and a lychee frozen into the middle of it, the oversized garnish in our undersized coupe glasses for the most popular basic bitch drink on our menu. There was exactly not enough alcohol in it, and people would order them just by pointing at one being carried to a table and saying, 'I want one of those.' The night crew were meant to freeze a tray of them as part of pack-down and they, well, just didn't.

'Am I meant to eighty-six the most popular drink?' he said, in response to my, 'Hi, how are you?'

'It's Monday lunch, people just drink wine. Don't stress. Just make a tray and it will be ready for dinner.'

'That's not the point. They didn't do their jobs.' He leaned back against the bar and ate a banana in frustration, completely unaware of how hilarious he looked. But I got it, we were no longer working as a team. We all lost the love. We had no common goal.

In my periphery, I saw a skinny body drowning in the kitchen uniform with his head down doing larder prep, and I knew who it was immediately. 'Hey, Baby Chef!'

He dropped his knife, walked out of the kitchen and gave me a hug so big, he picked me up off the ground. 'How the hell are you, Ho!' At least someone was happy to see me.

'Oh, you know, melting.'

'Tell me about it. Try working in the kitchen when it's forty degrees and the aircon doesn't make it to our end of the restaurant. I go through four t-shirts a day.'

'How's it been?'

'Shit. All the Thai chefs quit. At least I think they quit. I've been working doubles, back-to-back.' He was a skeleton.

'What happened?' I didn't have to ask. They'd been putting up with all the shit I had only just noticed for the entire time they had been working here, having their national dishes bastardised and being stripped of their voices. They either found new jobs or their self-respect.

Baby Chef looked around the room. 'I can't talk about it here. Wanna get a drink during break?' Something has gone down. 'I have to keep moving if we're going to open on time. Talk later, Ho.'

The set-up crew came in, and each of them was more deflated than the last. More people had quit. New restaurants were opening and offering our staff more money to do the same job, and they would even get knock-off drinks. I'd quit, too, if I were in their shoes. The old crew were tired from picking up after the very green, very underqualified and slow newbies. The heat was not the reason they moved at half pace.

'Don't bother learning their names, they quit as soon as they start. We've been on a hiring spree,' said Ev. 'We were so fucked the other night, I even had to help out in a section. I was terrible, but the newbie was worse.' Rough.

There are two kinds of Going Down in hospitality. The first version of Going Down is exactly what it sounds like. Picture a captain on a flight, panicking because the entire aircraft is making an accurately projected and swift descent into a mass of solid, immovable, jagged mountains. There are no parachutes on board, and no matter what you do, the outcome is always a bloody, painful death. That was the equivalent of the service I'd just worked through. The other version of Going Down is knowing that you're all going to crash and burn, but everyone's accepted death and is raiding the drinks cart while the captain's blasting music over the speakers on the way down. This is how we got through service prior to my holiday.

My shift was about to end and I cleaned up the screen on the reservation system while chugging a glass of water. Then, I heard a voice that was going to take all my pain away. 'How'd you go?' Night Host was in flats for once, rather than her signature Acne black pistol ankle boots.

'That was fucked. How long has it been like this?'

'A fortnight.'

'It's enough to make you quit,' I said. I quickly assessed Night

Host's face. 'But don't fucking quit on me.'

'Everyone's been poached. Or working here has scared them straight and they're going back to study.'

'Don't they need money?'

'Oh, they've all moved in with each other and are working part time. You've missed out on so much gossip.' The door to my vault creaked open. 'We also hired another host so the managers can float on the floor. She's a fashion student, but she's great. Quick. Smart. People treat her like she's an idiot so she takes advantage of it.'

'I like her already. I'm going to grab a drink with Baby Chef in his break. Did you want me to bring back any snacks for you?'

Night Host patted her bag. 'Thanks, but I'm sorted.'

I waited in the bar before it opened, chatting to the bartenders to see how they were going, and the sentiments were all the same. It didn't matter where you worked in the building, everyone was stretched thin.

Baby Chef texted me, 'Meet me at that bar in Collins Square. I don't want people to see me leave with you in case I get in trouble. Also, can you order me a burger? I think I'm going to run a few minutes late.'

I said my goodbyes to the bartenders and left via the basement exit. I made it to the end of the alleyway before someone grabbed my arm. It was Mike.

'Hey! You're back. Can we make a time to talk about my arts initiative?'

I had not thought about the strategy for his project since I last saw him.

'Yeah, sure. Do you want to come in an hour before a shift one day and we can run through it?'

'Actually, I'll send you a bunch of documents and show you the Facebook group I've started for it. I'll friend you and send you the page. Then you'll get an idea of what's up.'

'Yeah, cool. My privacy is on really high so we need at least a mutual friend for you to be able to see me. I'll find you. What's your last name?'

'Barker.'

'Oh, we already have a mutual friend. How do you know Bridget? I fucking love that woman.'

'I don't.' That was hard to believe. Everyone loved Bridget. Everyone had a crush on Bridget. Hell, even I had a crush on Bridget. 'She stole my girlfriend and moved overseas with her. We all used to work together.' That would do it.

As a person who was constantly being treated like an object that could be owned and was incapable of heartfelt, compassionate human interaction with anything attached to a penis, I explained to Mike that people in relationships could only be lost and not stolen.

'Yeah, but I'm still pissed off about it.' The poor guy wasn't just pissed, he was filled with love, but had nowhere to put it.

I sat in the bar waiting for Baby Chef as his burger slowly lost its heat and the fries wilted into a soggy mess.

'Hey, sorry I'm late. I couldn't get out of there. I had to show the new guy the section, so I've only got fifteen minutes before I have to be back.' He didn't even have time to change. He had thrown a t-shirt on over his work top and had runners on instead of his food-covered kitchen clogs.

'So, what the fuck is going on?'

'I don't really know. All the Thai guys got moved to the prep kitchen and I hear they're not coming back. It got really tense in the kitchen after you left and now we're all fucked.'

'Yeah. I'm hearing that from everyone. Don't you think it's a stupid idea to remove the Thai chefs and their faces from the kitchen when we're trying to sell authenticity?'

'The menu's changing.'

'I see ... and the Thai guys aren't happy about it?'

'Look, I don't understand what's happened. But there have been complaints and then people disappeared, and we're supposed to have new stuff on in a few weeks but there's no one to cook it.'

'How's the new food?'

'Yeah, nah.' Baby Chef inhaled all his food during that conversation and only stopped chewing to chug his beer. 'Hey, I'm sorry. I have to go. I'll see you tomorrow.' He gave me a greasy kiss on the cheek, put down forty dollars and ran out the door.

I was in shock. Shock from the weather, the sudden lack of stability at work, my sudden development of a conscience, the lack of clear information, the denial everyone was in, and the divisions between people at work. We were no longer one, big, mutually exhausted and dysfunctional family. We were broken, scattered across the city, anxious and unsure.

Welcome home, I told myself.

I went on Seek to look up all these new restaurants that were hiring. I scoffed as I scrolled through the ads and decoded their real-estate lingo for real meaning. I was a master at decoding these ads because me and everyone I knew had fallen victim to at least one or more of these phrases. I had even utilised a few myself when posting ads on job boards.

'New and exciting restaurant opening' means that the chef and owner have eaten at the country's 'best' (according to white-gaze lifestyle magazines) restaurants and stolen a dozen dishes to replicate poorly on their own menu. It could also mean that the chef and owner have gone overseas on a week-long eating trip and have decided that they're now the gatekeepers of that cuisine. Media will use phrases like 'reinvented' and 'elevated' to describe their watered-down versions of generational familial recipes that they have mutilated in the name of artistry and capitalism.

'Our latest venture' is code for one of two things: either the owners all need another business to launder money through, or the business is expanding way too quickly and won't last a year. Either way, it will be torture.

'Resilient' staff are always called upon when the executive chef or the general manager are tyrants, but always somehow keep their jobs because of their longstanding relationship with the owner. Or worse, they are the owner.

'Dedicated' means you will work more hours than you ever have in any other job, but you won't be paid for it because you'll be put on a seemingly attractive annual salary that will work out to be ten dollars an hour when you divide it by the hours you've worked.

'Buzzy CBD location' means that the owner's previous venture failed, so they are renovating and changing the name of the restaurant and nothing else. They hope you are too dumb to notice.

'Hardworking and energetic staff required' usually means that you'll be required to drink three cans of any energy drink on the market to perform your job. If you are burned out and say something about it, you'll be fired. More than one person will cry at the end of every shift. There is no staff meal, but you can order whatever you want off the menu at fifty per cent off.

'Hands-on owners' are generally people who have never worked in hospitality or completed any qualifications, but will micromanage everyone to the point where the customers think the venue is a giant mess. The 'hands-on owner' will also treat the restaurant as an extension of their living room and throw out everyone's cost of goods. They'll take prep from the bar and cool room to cater their own dinner parties.

'Award wages' is fancy speak for minimum wage. Management

will talk to you like you're lucky to work there and you will endure so much institutional abuse you will either break or become a bully. Tips will become very important to you and there will be numerous team meetings about honouring the pooling system instead of pocketing the tips from your section, even though you ate a lot of shit and kissed a lot of arse for those twenty dollars. There will be some weeks where you live off instant noodles.

'We promote from within' is another way to say that you'll be doing the job of someone with a much more senior title than you while being paid as a section waiter or a commis chef. Any changes that you implement to maximise efficiency or bring in more cash will be credited to your superior who comes in late every day and handballs half their jobs to you. When you do finally get offered a promotion, it will not pay as well as it used to and they'll argue that the new bonus structure they've put in place will mean your yearly salary is much higher. If you go to the trouble of working out the maths, you'll reailse that it isn't.

I didn't exactly work in the most professional environment, but I wouldn't bother leaving for something that might be worse. Everyone operates with the mentality of Better the Devil You Know. I definitely did. I'd already learned everyone's bad habits, weaknesses and strengths. I'd earned myself a permanent roster that worked with my lifestyle. I didn't want to start from zero all over again. The job ads all sounded so bleak. Once I ignored all the copy about the cuisine, décor and ownership, these venues were basically the same. I wondered how long my former colleagues could stand working in these restaurants. *They'll be back*, I thought to myself. And within a few months, most of them were. Better the Devil You Know.

Aside from the uncertainty and change of guard, work was basically the same, but my guilt went from simmering to a rolling boil. Every morning, I'd lie in bed, incapable of getting out of it without using all my willpower because I hated everything I had to do for the next eight hours. Every keystroke, every report, every person I walked through the door and every dollar I put through the till was a step towards cultural erasure, oppression, systemic racism, more fucking colonisation. I wasn't just a bad person, I was a bad Asian. And because all Asians look the same, one bad Asian makes us all look bad. And that Asian was me. But wokeness wasn't a thing back then. I couldn't verbalise why I felt the way I did, I just knew what I was doing was wrong.

Mike's arts initiative was something that distracted me from my daily tasks of cultural appropriation. He had a great idea, connections to emerging artists and exactly zero resources. Even if he didn't spend half the week working in the bar, he still needed more hands or more hours to make it happen. I figured that if I could help him spend the business's money on things that had nothing to do with food service, it was however many dollars less going towards racism and overhyped mediocrity.

'To get the first show up, we're going to need tracking on the walls so I can hang the art,' said Mike. He didn't know that Our Fearless Leader had already approved the spending for the tracking, but Our Fearless Leader wanted me to teach Mike how to ask for it.

'Cool, the thing with this company is, it doesn't spend money on stuff unless you can justify it. Are you giving the venue a cut of sales, are you getting bonus stock to sell over the bar, or are you guaranteeing more bodies in the bar to buy drinks to pay for the tracking?'

'Yeah.'

'But can you put it in writing? Verbalise your reach and the positive effects on the bar?'

'How do you mean?'

'Like an ROI.'

'What's that?' I looked at Mike in his leather jacket, combat boots, long t-shirt and torn black jeans. I had to speak his language. I opened my notebook and drew a graph.

'Ok, so, imagine you're a pimp. And you have a bunch of hookers. As a pimp, you have to take care of them. Clothe, feed, house, whatever. That's your base cost. They're your investments. Sorry, I should have explained. ROI stands for return on investment.'

Mike laughed and nodded. 'So, for each hooker, they have to bring in a certain amount of money every day, or week or whatever for you to justify being their pimp. And 'cause you're not a heartless bastard, you only take a cut because your hookers need money to live.'

'Right.'

'So, for example, you spend five hundred dollars a week per hooker.'

'Yep.'

'And you take, I dunno, forty per cent.' I start plotting the costs on the graph. 'Assuming the hooker charges fifty a handy, seventy a blowy and one-fifty for full-service, make an educated projection of how many services they will have to perform per evening before you make your five hundred back for the week. Everything after that is profit.'

'Yeah, but how hot is the hooker? That matters.'

'But you get what I'm saying, right? In this analogy, the tracking is the housing, feeding, clothing and the services rendered are the entry fee, bar sales or clip off the art works. But your ROI will be easier to explain because it's a one-time investment rather than ongoing.'

'Got it.'

'So, you'll have to put that together in an email for the tracking to be approved. It will take one launch party for the costs to be covered based on x people buying y drinks, or something. Do you have any contacts? I would probably suggest getting at least three quotes so Our Fearless Leader has an idea of how much it should cost. Also, negotiate with them to do it out of hours and get approximate timings on how long it will take. If it cuts into service time, I don't think they'll go for it. It's impossible, but aim for cheap, fast and good.'

'Like a hooker.'

'Yes, like a hooker.'

Mike grabbed my notebook. 'Do you mind if I take this for reference?'

I ripped the page out and handed it to him. 'All yours. I can't go back to the office with a page with the word "hooker" written all over it anyways.'

'Aren't you done for the day?'

'Yeah, but I don't want to take all my office shit home with me.'

'Well, I'm actually not working tonight. Want to get a drink? I wanna ask you more questions about this stuff.'

'Yeah, why not.'

We were the first people to walk into what was usually a late-night hospo bar, and one of the head bartenders was concentrating with every fibre of his being on pouring something brown into a smaller vessel of something brown with what appeared to be a piece of leather floating in it.

'Oi!' Mike jumped up to the bar and scared the shit out of the bartender.

'Ah, fuck! Now I have to start all over again.'

'What are you doing?'

'I'm making my entry for World Class.' We both moved closer to the bar. 'It's my take on the shoey. I cut a piece out of my old pair of Blundstones and I'm infusing it into this new local whisky, and I'll serve it like a take on the shoey. I don't know, I haven't fully fleshed out the concept, but it's cool, right?' Nope. Please throw this down the sink and start again. This was from a very highly awarded bartender, so either I wasn't getting something, or he'd lost the plot. I hate feet and I knew for sure I didn't want to put anything foot-adjacent into my mouth.

'I think I'm the wrong person to ask. You know me – martinis and shit beers. Tasteless and cold.'

'I'll give you a taste of it when I'm done. I want to see what you think.' Please don't.

'Yeah, it sounds cool, but is it food safe? It's your old shoe,' said Mike.

'I washed it, and I'll run it through a centrifuge.'

'But that just clarifies it, it doesn't get rid of all the bacteria you've hoofed in there.'

'I'll do some research. I'm just really into this idea of the reimagined, upscale shoey.'

We sat down and Mike explained how he knew some of the bartender's housemates. They were complaining about all the fruit flies he was bringing into the house with his experiments. All the free booze he brought home wasn't enough to offset the never-ending, pest-attracting trials. And if they happened to be home at the wrong time, they'd have to taste his creations.

'Why art?' I asked Mike. 'You're a bartender, and I want to say you study something full time ...?' I didn't even begin to pretend I knew him.

'I'm doing Entrepreneurship at RMIT.'

'And this arts initiative is your final exam thing?'

'Well, I don't know. It's a long story. I used to snowboard and I taught snowboarding until I got injured. My back is a wreck and I can't feel half the fingers in this hand.' Mike held up his dominant hand and I wondered why he spent his evenings slicing, shaking and stirring things with ice while handling money. 'And then I got into drinks, so I bartend. I like people, I like service. And now I like art and I want to do something cool with it. Art's a bit elitist and prohibitive so I just want to make it accessible. Not just to the public, but to young artists.' Mike spoke like a man who hadn't been crushed by the cruelness of reality yet. I would have been suspicious of his motives if his intentions weren't so clearly harmless. He had so much love and nowhere to put it. A man of the people. I wondered if this is what passion looked like.

'Hey, try this, guys.' The bartender put down full-sized pot glasses of his 'shoey' in front of us. 'The whisky isn't going to be ready for a while, but I've been making mead at home to go with it.' Judging from the lack of condensation, the mead was room temperature. Mike and I looked at each other with widened, terror-filled eyes. What did I do to deserve this? I chugged my mead as fast as I could, almost choking on the last gulp. Mike did the same. Our glasses were cleared, and we left before we were asked to try anything else. I opened my backpack and took out my bottle of water, flushed my mouth out and spat into the gutter.

'You want some?' I asked Mike, already handing him the bottle.

'Please.' He did the same. 'Food. We need food.'

It wasn't time to be picky. It was early enough that we managed to get a table without waiting in line at a cheap BYO Shanghainese restaurant that was a solid six-out-of-ten if you were sober. I laughed at the food order from the table next to us: two baskets of the same dumpling, chilli oil and peanut sauce wontons, and some fried noodles. Tourists. What a shit order.

Then one of the tourists spoke. 'Hey, how do you two know each other?' Evidently, I was friends with the shit orderers. I knew the sommelier from another restaurant in the city, and Mike used to work with both of them. One was his old boss.

'We don't,' I said. 'Not really. We work together.'

'Is this a date?'

'Fuck no,' we said in unison. 'But no offense,' we also said in unison at each other, and laughed.

'Okay, weirdos. Well, we brought all these wines to have on our night off with mates, but most of them have to work now. Want some?' I looked at what was open on their table. A vintage grower Champagne, a bottle of goldkapsel Riesling, and a Dauvissat that had half a glass left in it.

'What the fuck are you doing drinking those here?' I saw a few reds poking out of one of their bags, and I made the educated guess that they'd spent a week's pay on wine each.

'It's cheaper than ordering it at a restaurant. I bought these from work. BYO is only two-dollars-fifty a head here.'

'The food here is … fine, I guess. But you haven't even ordered the right stuff to go with the wine.'

'Everything goes with dumplings. Then we'll order some duck, or beef, or something to go with the reds. This place is the best, what are you talking about?'

There was a period where I forgot what good food tasted like because I always settled for what was open. My palate would crave too much sugar, fat and salt. I'd be chasing flavour bombs over balanced dishes because my body wanted a day's worth of seasoning condensed into one meal. I grew out of it, but some people grew used to it. In this situation, I couldn't tell who the wanker was – me or them?

'Thanks for the offer, and I know I'll regret it, but I'm done for drinking for the night.'

'I'll have some of the Chablis,' said Mike, and his old boss opened a box inside his bag. Inside were the restaurant series Riedels, some for the whites and some for the reds.

'I can't believe you brought your own glasses,' I said.

'If I am going to drink these wines, I want to taste them properly. Plus, the staff don't mind. It's not like they can tell me not to use my own glassware.' A waiter came over to take our order, and in our own completely silent, passive-aggressive Asian form of communication using only our eyes, we both said to each other, 'This is shit.'

Even though late-hours Chinese restaurants like this one were a service to the white-owned hospitality community, they didn't garner the same respect as other restaurants. My colleagues would know the names of everyone who worked in the venues that we frequented, and some basic information about their lives, but I bet these guys didn't care to know the name of one worker in this building. I wondered if they would have brought their own glassware without asking to any other restaurant.

I knew from the remedial Mandarin that I half-understood that our waiter wasn't related to the family who owned the restaurant. I knew she was one of thousands of kids whose parents spent their life savings to send her to Melbourne to study law, engineering, or whatever, and she was completely separated from her support network. I knew she was underpaid and this was the only job she could get because of her name, work history and language skills. I watched her being spoken to like she had a learning disability even though she understood fluent English. The importance of a wine glass and a plate of dumplings was being stressed to her in a tone I was all too familiar with. She nodded submissively because it was the role she was paid to play, and walked away. This was the cost of her parents' hope and her education.

There had been occasions when people would speak to me in the same manner, assuming by looking at me that I didn't speak English. I'd been asked if the restaurant name was inspired by my name, and how long I had lived in the country. I was spoken at in half-mime, half-shout. I knew I'd never grow out of it.

The industry teaches us that French cooking and French wines are superior, how to set a European-style table, the differences between a la carte and prix fixe, but it overlooks the skill involved in tempering spices, nixtamalising corn, fermenting cabbages or folding soup-filled dumplings. We are brainwashed into thinking that shoe-infused whisky will win a global cocktail competition and restaurants that can't afford a wine program don't deserve our respect. We have all fallen for the same lie and we have made ourselves intolerable.

I watched these well-honed palates celebrating the ability to drink their expensive wines with cheap Chinese food, as if they'd just tricked the owners who simply didn't know any better. I realised I didn't want to climb the ladder anymore. The top looked like a tone-deaf place to be.

9

'Dirty Playground,' said Mike over the phone.

'What?' I had my phone pressed between my ear and shoulder and was only half paying attention to him because I was trying to get through my front door.

'I'm calling my arts initiative Dirty Playground. I love the idea of a playground, 'cause it's all young, innocent and childish, and dirty 'cause it's gonna be dirty.'

I'd been working with Mike towards his first launch for a few weeks now and I became increasingly more than a sounding board for him. He would blurt out every little thought that came across his mind and would send me voice messages spelling out the word 'weather' like a cheerleader to tell me it was about to rain. Then he'd wait for me to tell him when the rain finally made it to my location so he could work out how far apart we were.

'It's wonderfully juvenile. I love it.' I unlaced my shoes and flopped on my couch.

'It's cool, not juvenile.'

'Porque no los dos?' We also communicated a lot in pop culture references.

I didn't realise that Mike had chipped away at me and we had become friends simply because he had no guard up. He'd basically forced me to care about him when he got off the phone to his parents one afternoon, rolled his jeans up to his knees, dangled his heavily tattooed chicken legs into the pool of my building as the sun was going down and unpacked his family drama. There's something vulnerable about a punk kid who shows you the whites of his knees and talks about his feelings. I didn't even realise it, but we'd been joined at the hip ever since.

Mike was what you'd call stereotypically handsome. He had dark hair, piercing blue eyes, a disgustingly radiant smile and he was covered in jobfuckers, so everyone at work had a crush on him. Jobfuckers are what I call tattoos that are visible outside the coverings of your clothing because they fuck your chances at a respectable job. And Mike didn't just have a floating tattoo here or there, he had heavily designed sleeves as well as tattoos on the back of his palms and the tops of his feet. If he made eye contact with any female for longer than three seconds, someone would have to mop up underneath her. Among certain circles, he was also known as Magic Mike.

Everyone at work also thought we were fucking, because unlike everyone else in the building, who treated me like I was prickly, Mike would jump on my back or pick me up off the floor every day he walked into work as a hello. And I was cool with it. If you ever saw a punk kid happy to see someone and a historically stand-offish person not tell the happy punk, 'No touching,' you'd probably think the same thing, too. Admittedly, we were both getting around quite a bit at this stage of our friendship, but we were fucking everyone except each other. Whenever we would catch up to debrief on the missing hours of our evenings, Mike would start the conversation with, 'You had cock coming at you from all directions,' turn his hands into puppets and finish with 'Cock, cock, cock, cock, cock,' while pecking at my shoulders like a rooster. We had reputations for being alternative and open-minded, but our relationship still confused everyone.

Mike would pick me up from work or turn up at my apartment, asking me for my thoughts on logos, copy for his launch, assistance in writing a media release, identifying appropriate media, how to approach journalists and determining profit percentage. In the end, I was doing half of it for him while we sat in my apartment eating take out and drinking heavily. I refused to go to his apartment after I pointed out how much vaginal fluid was on his couch. I couldn't find a place to safely sit. He also lived in one of those weird shitbox studios where there were cracks in the walls, the roof was shifting, there was no airflow, you had to walk through the shower to get to the toilet and everything was either mouldy, squishy or literally shitty. There was a huge difference between what we each deemed acceptably hygienic, and I considered his apartment a health hazard.

In these weeks, Mike realised he couldn't do Dirty Playground on his own. When he asked me if I'd be his partner for the initiative, it was the first time I had ever seen him be coy. With our friendship, I'd assumed I'd be doing the work anyways, so this was a way for me to at least have part-ownership in something that wasn't hospitality related. I was sick of letting my job define me, and even though I knew it would be a long time before either of us would see a dollar from the initiative (it was the arts, after all), at least it was another industry. One that I could risk being new to, ignorant about and shit at.

We made it official by signing contracts over martinis in my favourite dank bar, which turned out to be one of Mike's previous places of employment. We worked out that we had probably been in the same room countless times, but never met. Mike would also dig up a photograph of us both at an event held by one of my friends, who was another of Mike's previous employers, called the Aphrodisiac Orgy. This was a legitimate event that was part of the Melbourne Food and Wine Festival, and I had been called in to play Jesus at a blasphemous version of the Last Supper due to my shaved head. I wore a crown of thorns and a robe made of clingwrap, and Mike was walking around with a tray of drinks, topless with a ball gag in his mouth. There was also a naked guy who was shucking oysters all afternoon, a naked woman who had sushi eaten off her, a goth guy who did the steamiest of pole dances, and an actual orgy happened in the back room. Understandably, neither of us remembered each other from the event, but Mike determined from the photographic evidence that our friendship was fate. He may have looked like a tough nut on the outside, but on the inside, he was all love, light, feelings and all that other hippie shit.

Mike had an excellent eye for talent. The artists he picked out are now all wildly successful, even though I had my doubts about a few of them. But I stayed out of it because it was not my area of expertise. Our division of labour was that he dealt with the artists and I did all the back-end stuff. Aside from having no taste, I did not have it in me anymore to deal with precious egos and wild, nonsensical demands.

The first artist we launched was a teenager from Springvale who specialised in street art. After hanging his show, printing out all the price lists, photographing the work, bumping in the sponsored booze and doing all the pre-launch stuff, we went back to mine for a knock-off drink. Mike bought a bottle of gin for our efforts and he taught me how to properly make a martini. I didn't have any of the equipment at home, so we cowboyed it with a pair of chopsticks and a couple of vacuum flasks that I'd previously used exclusively for herbal soups.

'It doesn't matter if you have good ice or shit ice, you have to watch the dilution,' he said, stirring his flask. 'And always taste it before you serve it. If someone serves you a drink without checking it first, it's not going to be balanced. Not even the best bartender in the world could eyeball it.' He stuck his chopstick in my flask and tasted it. 'You need to stir it more. And for your taste, add more vermouth.'

I'd successfully made my first martini, and Mike had single-handedly ruined the bottom line for a few bars across the city.

'I can only stay for one,' he said. 'I have to go to my brother's birthday and I need to drive 'cause it's in Brunswick and I've got my gear in the back of my car.'

'Oh nice, what's he doing?'

'It's just a bunch of his friends hanging out at the skate park. They've brought beers and some snacks. I think there are food trucks or something.'

'Oh, cool.' Of course, Mike liked to skateboard. Even though snowboarding was off the cards for him because it literally broke his body, he would rationalise that a board with wheels in a concrete square would be safer because he wouldn't be flying through the air and landing flat on his back on deceptively compact ice. 'What time are we getting to the bar tomorrow?'

'Three, to be safe? I think if we finish early, we get some food and go back to the launch.'

'Good idea.'

A few hours later, Mike called. Mike never called. We were on strict texting terms, so I knew something was up.

'Is everything okay?' There was heavy breathing and a voice in the background that I couldn't make out.

'Um, I'm gonna come to yours. Is that okay?'

'Sir, hang up the phone, now.'

'Mike? Mike, can you hear me?'

The call cut out. I rang back but it went straight to voicemail. I didn't have Mike's brother's number so I couldn't check in on him. I texted Mike but he didn't immediately respond like he usually did. Something was wrong.

An hour later, my intercom buzzed. Mike was at my door.

'Can I come up?' I didn't say anything, just buzzed him in. He knocked on my door incessantly until I opened it.

'What the fuck is wrong with you now?' I asked.

He looked perfectly fine. He wasn't beaten up, bloody or wasted. He had all his fingers, his keys, his phone and his wallet. I was relieved but unimpressed.

'I just lost my licence.'

'What!' We had to install a blank canvas the next day, as the artist was going to do a live mural as part of the launch, and we were relying on Mike's tank of a car to pick up the boards.

'It doesn't kick in immediately, so I can pick up my car and drive it home, but I lost my licence.'

'What happened?'

'So, we were at the skate park and I only had a beer and a half. There were chips and stuff, so it wasn't on an empty stomach. We skated the whole time. I couldn't be drunk to do that.' I looked at Mike's slender frame. Even though we both held Responsible

Service of Alcohol certificates in order to do our jobs, Mike's body was hospitality calibrated, which meant he was a highly functional drunk. There was no way he would be able to gauge his level of inebriation like a regular person. 'Then I left because we have to get ready for the show tomorrow and I got pulled over. I was calling you to let you know what was going on, but the cop saw that my phone was out so I turned it off so he wouldn't fine me. I blew point-zero-five.'

'That's not the end of the world.'

'They were actually really nice about it.' Mike always gave people the benefit of the doubt. He had a softness to him that made even cops be kind to him – or maybe it was because he was a well-spoken, hot, white male. 'I told them I only had a beer and a half and they said I could ride around with them for half an hour. We were hoping my blood alcohol level would go down and they could let me drive home.'

'I'm guessing that didn't happen.'

'I ended up blowing point-zero-six.'

'Shit.'

'Yeah, they were like, "You do know what happens now? We're really sorry about it." They apologised to me!'

'So why didn't they take you home?'

'I asked them to take me here. It's not like I can drive anymore. Let's finish that bottle of gin.'

'What are we gonna do about the mural boards?'

'I asked one of my friends to pick it up. He actually offered to help install it since we don't know shit about building things.'

'Excellent, 'cause if I can't staple it or tape it, I call a professional. I am useless.'

'Wait. Do you have a licence?'

'No. Are you kidding? I let my learners lapse.'

'I can teach you to drive.'

'No you can't,' I said, gesturing to his wallet. 'I'm an aggressive pedestrian. Could you imagine me in charge of a machine with an engine? It's safer this way. Plus, I drink too much.'

We finished off the entire bottle of gin and, unsurprisingly, neither of us got alcohol poisoning and we woke up without hangovers. We had clearly been spending too much time together. I woke up on one end of the couch and Mike was on the other, threatening to touch me with his greyed, stained socks. Mike rubbed his eyes open and said, 'Mind if my friend picks me up from here?'

I gave him a spare toothbrush and a towel, stirfried some noodles for breakfast and sent him on his way.

When I arrived at the bar, I had to enter through the restaurant because it was an hour before any bartender was going to prep for open. The Restaurant was heaving. I'd forgotten that it was a non-stop flood of people as soon as the doors opened on the weekend – or rather, I'd buried the memory of having to push through weekend services. I said hi to the host on duty and started walking down the stairs when a regular grabbed my arm. I hated when customers touched me.

'What are you doing here on a weekend?' It seemed the weekend didn't stop him wearing his ill-fitted finance-bro suit-and-tie get-up. I didn't even know the name of this guy, but he was always the first person in on a Monday or Tuesday, acted like he made more money than he did, ate curry without rice and never tipped. He also had a terrible habit of thinking that women needed to be physically touched by him. I stared at his hand on my arm until he finally got the hint and let go.

'Bumping in a show.' I didn't even talk to his face, just stared at his hand hovering dangerously close to my arm again.

He reached for the inside of my elbow. 'What show?'

I decided that because I wasn't working, I didn't need to be nice to him. So many Men think that because your job involves being nice to them, you're flirting. Not today, Satan.

'I need to go.'

'Wait.' He grabbed my forearm.

'What is this? Who are you? What's going on, here?' Mike. Thank god. He chopped his way into the conversation by hacking the guy's arm away from me. 'Away with you! Back to your table. Back!' He waved the finance bro away with both arms, the sliders from the zips on his leather jacket jingling with every movement.

'Seriously, Jess. You can't look any more like a lesbian and yet, cock. Cock coming at you from all directions!' Mike turned his hands into rooster heads again and jabbed at my shoulders all the way down to the bar.

I double-checked the menus, catalogues and numbers were still where I'd hidden them and sat in a booth watching two men in their twenties build a space for a triptych out of nothing. My only job was to go out and get a sponge to hold one of the boards in place in case it buckled under the janky frame they'd hammered together. It didn't matter anyway because I ended up buying the work, and that fifty-cent sponge is still holding the entire piece together.

'So, what's going on here?' One of the waiters decided to eat his staff meal in the bar.

'It's for the launch tonight.'

'No, not the launch. I mean you and Mike.' I saw him eyeing off the guys as they matched up pieces of wood and wiped sweat off their brows.

'Nothing.'

'I don't believe you.'

'Hmm, think of it like Liza and Halston.'

'Mike's gay, loves sex and cocaine? Just my type.'

'Hahaha. No. As in we are more than friends and less than lovers.'

'A shame.' He picked around the chicken wing floating in his bowl.

'For you or for me?'

'For the entire gay millennial community in Melbourne. But sexuality's a spectrum, am I right?' He winked at me and turned around to go upstairs. 'Don't eat the staff meal, by the way.'

'I'm not working, but noted.'

Within a week, rumours that Mike and I were fishing off the company pier had been dispelled, and every second person came to me for their blessing to have a crack at Mike. 'Go forth and bone, my child,' I'd say, marking a cross in the air with my index and middle finger. I prided myself on being an excellent wingman.

The launch was done in two hours. All the sponsored booze was drunk, all the artworks sold, the artist was happy and so was Mike. It didn't matter which way we looked at it, it was a success. The bar was packed and all the people who came for free booze were opening their wallets. Next launch, I'd get our stuff printed and paid for by The Restaurant. Baby steps.

'Let's celebrate,' said Mike, eyes as wide as saucers and with a big, toothy grin. I didn't even get a chance to respond before he dragged me around the room to make sure we put red dots on everything, removed all the catalogues so people didn't call us wanting to buy works that weren't for sale, and counted the cash deposits. 'I negotiated that we keep the deposits, and the artist gets the rest.'

'That's fair considering it's the first show we've put on. Have we covered all our upfront costs?'

'Let's just say our hooker is smokin' hot.'

'Excellent.'

Mike unzipped my breast pocket, crammed a wad of cash in there and said, 'Come,' to me, like he was training a puppy. We walked a few blocks to another bar he used to work at, and a staff member greeted him with a tray of shots.

'Hey, man, how did the launch go? Sorry I couldn't be there, but ...' he gestured to his place of employment.

'Hi, I'm Jess,' I said while picking up the shot glass.

The staff member cheered. 'You're Jess! Nice to finally meet you.' He was also a hugger. He led us to a space behind the courtyard that only high-functioning alcoholics from the 101 Collins building knew about.

'Sorry, I know it's full of wankers, but it's the only space we've got that's not booked.'

'It's great. Don't worry.' Mike waved to more of the staff behind the bar. If I knew the majority of people who worked on the floor in CBD restaurants, Mike knew all the bartenders. If we weren't careful, we could potentially lose the next twelve hours.

Mike pointed to the middle of the room where a bunch of rhythmless white guys were attempting to dance, but ended up looking like overcooked pasta being waved about in the air.

'Isn't that the arsehole who was talking to you before the bump-in?'

'I can't tell. They all look the same.' Every single one of them had floppy hair, broken capillaries across their cheeks, ties stuffed in their blazer pockets and the top button of their shirts undone, and none of them could find the beat to Iggy Azalea's *Fancy*. It was an embarrassment to watch. 'I can't look anymore.'

Mike laughed, shielding his eyes from them in his periphery and said, 'One drink and we are out. This is so not our scene right now.'

We sat patiently, aware that the bar crew were in the weeds, going down hard. The bussies couldn't buss fast enough and orders were getting lost.

'Should we do it?' I asked.

'I think we have to.'

We both got up out of our chairs, grabbed a tray each, filled it with glassware, and I followed Mike behind the bar.

'We're gonna do some glasses for you boys,' Mike said to his old colleagues.

'Thank fuck. Our POS system keeps disconnecting so we are drowning. Everyone's writing manual tickets, we can't read anyone's handwriting and adding up bills is a bitch.'

We polished eight racks of glasses, found new batteries for the bar's well-hidden calculator that was sticky with juice, and were thanked with a bottle of Champagne. We refused glassware because the bar needed all the glasses they could get. Instead we stood in the corner, necking wine straight out of the bottle, passing it back and forth like kids on a stoop at a house party. We felt like kings, but most definitely looked like wankers.

One of the floppy-haired fuckwits came over and started clicking his fingers in front of my face. 'Door girl.'

There is a moment when a civilian sees a hospitality worker outside of their professional environment. It could be a barista, a waiter, a bartender, a media-darling chef, or even a door girl. There are two options for the civilian. The first, which is the most respectful, is to acknowledge the hospitality worker (a wave is enough) and leave them alone to enjoy their night off. The second, the painfully awkward and potentially destructive option, is to walk up to the out-of-context hospitality worker and try to have a conversation with them as if they're your friend, even though you've only ever treated them like a servant.

'Oi, door girl!' He kept clicking his fingers at me. Mike leaned in close to my ear and whispered, 'I think it's a different guy.' It was almost the same guy, except this one was about ten years older and wearing a tailored Brioni suit, which meant he was probably a few pay brackets higher than Young Finance Bro.

'She has a name,' Mike said to Old Finance Bro, and Old Finance Bro ignored Mike completely. Old Finance Bro had made a huge mistake, because for all the love and light that Mike put into the world, if you disrespected him in the slightest way, he would make it his life's mission to end you. Mike believed in karma like every other touchy-feely spiritual person, but he only believed in it because he made sure that he was the one to deliver it.

'So, door girl, my friend there just got engaged and we are

going to Vegas for the bachelor party.'

'That's gross. I hope you all get STIs and lose all your money.'
I wasn't being paid to be nice to these people and we were not at
work. I had nothing on the line.

'You're funny, door girl. Anyways, I was wondering, if we paid
for your ticket and your accommodation, do you want to come
with us?'

'No.'

'A free ride,' he gyrated his hips, still missing the beat, 'You're
saying no to a free ride?'

'Getting raped is actually quite costly.'

'Okay, enough of this. Who are you? What are you doing?
What are you trying to do here?' Mike stood in between us,
getting all up in the face of the Old Finance Bro. I watched him
slip his thumb over the mouth of the Champagne bottle and start
to shake it up. 'Honestly, what are you trying to do here?'

'I'm just asking if the door girl wants to go on holiday with us.'

'She already said no.'

'She doesn't mean it.'

Mike shook the bottle one more time, raised it to Old
Finance Bro's face and moved his thumb. An explosion of
Champagne went into Old Finance Bro's face and all over his
five-thousand-dollar suit. 'Now back off,' Mike said, leaning in
really close to his face.

The bar was so busy that no one noticed what happened. Old

Finance Bro tried to complain to the bartenders, but they all played dumb and handed him a stack of napkins to clean himself up.

'We said one drink and out. I'd say that's our one drink.' Mike grabbed my hand, pushed a button, and the sliding door to the venue's bins opened into an alleyway.

'What a giant cockburger,' Mike said, walking ahead of me. And then he stopped and turned around, arms close to his body like a T-rex, hands held up like sock puppets, and then he lunged for me. 'But honestly, cock! Cock coming at you from all directions. Cock, cock, cock, cock, cock!' If my body wasn't so conditioned to getting hit, I probably would have woken up with bruises from all his rooster pecks.

Monday crept up on me after celebrating a little too hard. Mike hadn't slept at his since his licence had been suspended, so I conceded and gave him a set of keys in case I ever lost mine, or he needed to be away from his hovel of mould.

'I need to drive my car home before I can't,' said Mike to me when I came back from the gym.

'It's still there? How many parking fines do you think you have?'

'Fines? I'll be lucky if it hasn't been impounded.' As it happened, Mike was a ridiculously lucky man. His car had been ignored for the entire weekend. It was a close call, though. He was about to cop a fine as he ran up to his car, but managed to charm his way out of it because the parking inspector hadn't printed the ticket yet. It must be nice to be both lucky and ridiculously good-looking.

My usual routine of meticulously doing my laundry and organising myself for the week didn't happen, so I was forced to dress like a normcore, middle-aged white man: a white t-shirt, faded jeans and a pair of boots. It was fine. It was a step up from what most people wore for work, which ranged from booty shorts that would ride so far up someone's camel toe that there was risk of pubic hair escaping, or t-shirts with their sleeves cut off so extremely you could see nipple piercings and bad-decision torso tattoos (technically not a jobfucker if the shirt was whole).

When I got into work, there was a note stuck on the host desk's computer screen. It was a list of last-minute VIPs I had to put into the system. As I stood there, booting up the computer, entering names and adding additional notes to their preferences, the CFO walked in carrying a clipboard. He was always flustered, having spent the last five years of his employment feverishly shifting money and chasing down the owner.

'Is the owner here yet?'

'I'm the only one in the building right now.' I didn't even look at the CFO, just kept typing and making sure I was adding people to the right days.

'You know, you have exceeded my expectations.'

'Of what?'

'Well, look at you.' The CFO eyed me up and down. He made

me want to have a shower immediately. 'Who would have known you would help the company make so much money?'

'Does that mean you're going to give me a raise?'

'I'm not, um, no. I, ah, I'll just sit down over there and wait for the owner. Could I trouble you for a coffee?' The audacity.

'It's getting serviced this morning and I don't know how to make coffee.' It was a half-lie. I was technically taught, but I never practised my skills. I'd gone my entire food service career without having to make a coffee and I wasn't going to start now. I'd make the kitchen black coffees, but as soon as someone asked me to spin milk, I'd say, 'I won't do that because I like you as a person and you've done nothing to deserve that kind of punishment.' Then I'd pour them some cold milk on the side. I relished in the CFO's slow, awkward shuffle to the booth the furthest away from me, sitting in complete silence and waiting for his master.

I set myself up at the corner of the bar, plugged in my laptop and started my week.

'Eh-ohhhhhhhh!' I almost fell off my stool. It was Mike – a fresh, showered and changed version of him. 'Bet you didn't expect to see me here.'

'Definitely not this soon.'

'I'm covering for Ev. He's sick.' He turned on the coffee machine and started opening fridges and freezers to check the stock. 'Let's set this bitch up!'

He looked over at the CFO. 'Who's this guy?' I forgot that

most of the crew had never met the team from the office.

'Finance department. Here to meet the owner.'

'I'm assuming there's a reason why you haven't offered him water and coffee.'

'You assume correctly.'

'Hey. You. I'm making myself a coffee, do you want one?'

The CFO was shocked out of his trance over nothing and said, 'Um, yes. I mean, the machine is getting serviced? But yes. A flat white.'

'It won't taste the best but it will be fine.' Mike smiled at me and started whacking, grinding, pushing buttons and steaming milk. He didn't stop steaming milk. The jug was hissing and spluttering, which meant Mike had taken it too far. He smiled again at me.

'Sugar?'

'Ah, yes, please.'

Mike set the coffee up on a saucer with sugar, a teaspoon and even found a stale cookie in one of the drawers that the staff set away for their own snacking. He carried the set to the CFO on a tray. He looked the CFO directly in the eye and said, 'Enjoy.' What he was really saying to him was *I most definitely hope this is the most unenjoyable coffee you've ever tasted.*

Back at the bar Mike lowered his voice. 'I burned that coffee to shit and that milk is basically curdled. He's going to desperately want a glass of water and I'm going to make him come up here to get it.' Karma, delivered yet again, by Mike. In the distance, I heard a splutter and laughed quietly to myself. I smiled at Mike and he smiled back at me while slicing up fruit for service with his back turned to the restaurant.

'Excuse me,' a voice called in the distance.

Mike kept his back turned.

'Excuse me?'

Mike continued cutting.

The CFO sat there for a minute before he realised the restaurant wasn't open and he could walk up to the bar.

'Could I please get another sugar?'

'Oh, yeah, hey. Didn't hear you over there. Here you go.' Mike handed him three sticks and continued on with his prep.

'You were right about the machine needing servicing.' Small victories.

Because of all the VIPs, we were unusually busy for lunch service. The VIPs didn't have a sense of urgency about them because the majority of them were DNBs (Do Nothing Bitches, which meant they didn't have jobs), so we couldn't turn their tables. This meant that a lot of the regulars ended up sitting around the communal table or the bars.

'Are you sure you can't sit me at a table?' said one of the regulars, who thought that occasionally spending almost a thousand dollars was insurance to preferential treatment. What he didn't know was all these VIP-DNBs had already spent more than that on wine alone.

'I'm sorry, but if I could, I would. I can always start you at the bar and move you to a table as soon as one becomes available.' I led him to the bar with his guest, who was also a regular, though I had never seen them dine together before. The other regular would always come in by himself with a book, drink water, have a single dish for lunch and required almost no attention. The service that these two regulars expected were on opposite ends of the spectrum, so I concluded that this was a working lunch.

'Hey, dude at the bar is allergic to peanuts, right?' One of the senior waiters had just been promoted to manager, so he was running his first service as Mr Manager and being overly cautious and diligent with the guests.

'Yep. But he insists he isn't anaphylactic. Just mark the dishes again, just in case. Oh, and I said I'd move him to a table once one becomes available. Two-pax.'

'Easy.'

High-maintenance Regular ordered his food through Mike. I flagged the docket for a peanut allergy and let Mike know in case of cross-contamination with anything in the bar.

'Hey, is a table ready yet?' said High-maintenance Regular as I was warning Mike.

'No one has asked for the bill yet, so it will be a while off. You're the first to be seated at a table, should one become available.'

'Oh, I don't mind sitting up here,' said Laid-back Regular. 'It's fine. We aren't going to be here for long anyways.'

'Someone's just asked for the bill, so we can move you soon,' said Mr Manager, after running up to the bar.

'Don't worry about it. I'm happy,' insisted Laid-back Regular.

'Are you happy?' asked Mr Manager, turning to High-maintenance Regular.

'Me? Happy? I won't be happy until Jess fucks me,' he said, leaning back a little and laughing. Laid Back Regular screwed up his face and looked down.

'Nope,' I said. 'I am not serving you ever again.'

High-maintenance Regular scoffed like we were all there for his amusement.

'I'll deal with this,' said Mr Manager. A food runner came up behind the regulars and dropped their dishes. They weren't sharing plates despite neither of the dishes containing peanuts, so they definitely were not friends. Laid-back Regular didn't pick up his cutlery to eat, and I left Mr Manager there to sort out the mess. I didn't want to be anywhere near them.

I stood at the till processing bills that were finally coming in. A few minutes later Mr Manager came up behind me.

'Are you cool to finish the rest of your shift or do you want to leave?'

'I'm fine. I just want to crush up a few peanuts and put them in his food.'

'Don't go to the back end of the restaurant. I've got it. I won't let him talk to you again. Cool?'

'Thanks.' As we were having the conversation, Our Fearless Leader walked in because he'd heard all these VIPs were in for lunch. He fluttered around the restaurant fluffing everyone up and stopped by the bar to say hello to the regulars. Then he made a beeline across the restaurant towards me.

'What did you say to the guy at the bar? He said you were very rude to him and he won't dine here again.'

'Me? I didn't say anything. He said he wouldn't be happy until I fucked him and I said I would never serve him again. Mike, Mr Manager, the food runner and every other guest in the vicinity heard if you need to ask anyone about it.' Our Fearless Leader turned on his heel and I watched him speaking to everyone I'd mentioned. Then he dragged High-maintenance Regular outside, though we had full view of them through the windows. High-maintenance Regular started spitting and sputtering angrily. He waved his arms in the air and stormed off.

'I've banned him from The Restaurant,' Our Fearless Leader said once he was back inside. 'Comp the bill.'

'For how long?'

'Forever,' he replied.

Within a few weeks the regular was back. Dining, splurging and harassing women on the tables close to him like nothing had happened. But I only heard about it, because he was never there during my shifts. Clearly the company didn't think I was worth as much as a plate of fried rice, a bottle of Clare Valley Riesling and a couple of watered-down vodka cocktails.

'How are we going to stop all this cock coming at you from all directions?' said Mike, when I told him the arsehole regular was back.

'Peanuts.'

'I'm not going to kill the guy, even though I'd like to. I know I make fun of cock coming at you all the time, but it is not a good thing. Men are shit. Just stick with me.'

I did.

10

I didn't give The Restaurant any more of me after discovering that Old Man Sexual Harasser was officially back as a regular. I stuck it out for a few months, but eventually I quit. I didn't quit dramatically or emotionally. I resigned to Our Fearless Leader after a weekly profit and loss meeting where we were urged to strive for more money while spending less. He simply responded with, 'I understand.'

I gave them six weeks.

Through existing relationships, I ended up in a partnership that toured massive wine events across the country, designed to appeal to consumers rather than to trade. We wrangled winemakers from Australia and New Zealand, treating them like rock stars on trips across the country. We set up, poured wine, packed down, gorged ourselves on food and drink, jumped on planes and did it all again. The winemakers loved it because in their day-to-day lives they were simply a very specific type of farmer. Winemaking, much like working in a restaurant, is backbreaking, Sisyphean, thankless, and romanticised by rich cunts just enough to trick whole new generations into joining the industry.

The idea was to run the events in a varietal or region-specific trade-tasting format with around sixty producers per event. This would create a platform for winemakers to sell direct to the consumer, rather than through a third party like a bottle shop or a restaurant. In reality, it became a huge piss-up event for ticketholders and we'd have to hire DJs and food trucks to keep the energy up, as well as making sure no one died of alcohol poisoning. For the winemakers, it was like going on Spring Break. They'd be smashing cans of beer while pouring their juice to punters and receiving positive feedback directly, rather than getting a series of noes from meticulously honed palates that couldn't help crunching numbers and looking at what else was similarly listed. Winemakers could be away from the elements, rubbing shoulders with their peers, swapping stories, engaging with potential lifelong customers and hearing neverending yeses.

Many emotional, intoxicated strangers cried on me during these events. I held a lot of hair back in toilets, and on one occasion at a five-hundred-person event, I ended up with an entire wheelie bin's worth of spittoon gargle on me, plus the claggy, rehydrated kitty litter used to soak up the half-swallowed wine. The lining for the spittoon had split because a drunken ticketholder had thrown their broken wine glass in the bin, and it ruptured when I went to swap it out. When I was covered in the mouth-juice of hundreds of strangers after sweating through an entire day's work, I felt like Liam Neeson in *Taken* when he mouth-breathed down the phone to a stranger. *I have a particular set of skills, skills that I have acquired over a very long career, skills that make me a nightmare for people like you. I will look for you, I will find you, and I will kill you.* The skills that I'd acquired did not involve hand-to-hand combat, but they did involve looking through ticket purchases, viewing security tape and being so social-media literate that I could probably intercept the glass-chucker at their dinner table, wring my clothing out into their wine glass and force them to drink it in front of me. It was a shame that after breaking down the venue, I only had a handful of hours to hose myself off, sleep, pack and make it to the airport. The Mike Barker brand of karma would have to wait.

While on the road, we treated it like touring a festival. The winemakers were tied to us as the main act but were encouraged to do extra events and tastings in every city, like sideshows. Those who didn't have sideshows leaned on me to have a group dinner organised or a list of places they could check out. Somehow, I went from partner to fixer and tour guide. While people's needs were different, one common request amongst winemakers was not amazing food, a chill atmosphere, or a particular type of cuisine that is hard to find in their region – it was that the venue would accommodate BYO. This was partly because there are very different sets of requirements for a wine list depending on whether you ask a sommelier or a winemaker, and they both believe they are right. Think of them like the ultimate industry frenemies. A lot of, but not all, winemakers also cringe at paying the restaurant mark-up on wine they know the landed unit cost for (or have had a hand in making while doing vintage overseas). The only solution to this problem was to send them to wine bars with extensive cellars where only a flat fee would be added to the retail price to drink in and where all the food would inevitably be the same, or to negotiate a hefty corkage fee with the manager at a restaurant that did not normally offer BYO. It was a huge pain and it made me feel like an entitled jerk.

I sat through a few of these dinners before it felt like *Groundhog Day*. After that I resigned myself to hanging out in my room with a piece of fruit for the rest of the tour, debriefing with Mike.

'Why aren't you partying with the rest of them?'

'I can't do it. My body is saying no. How the hell do these forty-plus-year-old farmers with really fucked-up bodies keep backing it up?'

'Deprivation. Remember, you said it was Spring Break!' Mike emphasised Spring Break like Kitty Sanchez from *Arrested Development*. 'You're just topping up, they're starting from zero.'

'Then wouldn't that mean that I have trained my body to withstand this kind of behaviour? Anyways, I can't eat another charcuterie plate, cheese plate or polenta chip, along with very expensive wines my palate has not learned to appreciate yet.'

'But do you like the taste?'

'Yeah, but I don't know what I'm tasting or why I like it. It just seems like a waste. Plus, when all you drink are awesome wines, when you have something that's only "very good", you think it's shit.'

'You're a wanker, but you don't know why you're a wanker. Oh, cry me a river. At least you're consistent, I'll give you that.'

'Plus, I miss food with flavour.'

'Like what? Cheese has flavour. Salami has flavour.'

'Asian food. Any Asian food. I want noodles, I want offal, I want crisp, charred, sweet vegetables kissed by a wok. I want fermented tofu melted over morning glory. I want herbal soup with tofu skins and chicken feet. I want silken tofu with raw garlic and century egg. I want a crisp and lacy banh xeo with plump-arse prawns, immaculate lettuce, herbs and nuoc mam. I want a stinky bamboo salad. I want a fermented fish som tum so spicy I see through time, and sticky rice to sop it up with. I want a cauldron of kimchi stew. I never crave cheese platters, but I always crave Asian food.'

'Why don't you go get some take-out?'

'I don't know what's good here. I'd rather just eat raw fruit and vegetables than face disappointment. I couldn't handle another disappointment.' The night before, I'd been tricked into going to a Sichuan restaurant recommended by a non-Chinese person that only hit the spicy note of the six basic flavours of Sichuan cuisine.

The food was a caricature of the region. It angered my being and shattered my soul. What a waste of a meal.

'You're obsessed with reading reviews and going online to stalk venues. Surely there's a decent place around you.'

'I don't trust reviewers. And I especially don't want white reviewers to tell me what good non-white food is. How do they even know what they're tasting? This is how we ended up with lines outside of work, remember?'

'Ha. Good point. When are you back?'

'I have seven meals of white bread and beige left.'

'I was asking about the time, but okay. Let's go out and eat when you're back.'

'Sold.'

As soon as I got home, I dumped all my clothes in the washing machine, not bothering to separate my blacks from my delicates, put some rice on to cook and gave myself a good scrub. I only managed to put underwear on before I emptied a can of black bean fried dace onto the fluffy white grains and inhaled it all without taking a breath. I'd officially become my grandfather, I just needed to swap my black crop top for a stained, no-longer-white wifebeater. When he wasn't sucking the collagen off the steamed barramundi's head at a family banquet, my grandfather was chewing on canned Chinese preserved fish. I made a mental note to throw some into my bag for the next tour.

I heard a jingle of keys and Mike appeared in my apartment.

'Eyyyy! Welcome back!' He picked me up off the floor to give me a hug. His cold leather jacket pressed against my skin, and the harder he squeezed me, the more the teeth of his zippers bit me. 'Are you eating before we go out for food?' He stared at my empty, oil-slicked bowl.

'I had to.'

'Baby Chef, Camilla and Shiteater are coming, too.'

'Awesome. That means I can order more.'

Mike stepped back and looked at me. 'How are you smaller after only eating meat and cheese?'

'I just lost my appetite.'

'Let's get you fat,' he said, poking my belly. 'Hey, look at this.' He took one arm out of his leather jacket, rolled up the sleeve of his t-shirt and flexed. 'You've inspired me. I'm working on my glamour muscles.'

Underneath the years of ink, I saw the formation of muscle definition. 'Shaking cocktails not enough for you?'

'Nah. I wanna get ripped. Feel it. C'mon, feel it.' I gave his bicep a squeeze between my thumb and index finger.

'Mine are harder.' Mike squeezed my arm with his free hand.

'I'm gonna beat you.'

'Yeah?'

'Yeah.'

'Now, let's go accumulate some mass.'

We went to one of the fancier Chinese restaurants in the city, in part because the stereotypical, self-referential décor mimicking what white people thought an emperor's court looked like, made our non-Chinese industry friends think it was somehow cleaner or better than a fluorescent-light fishbowl, but also 'cause they were pretty decent considering we didn't have to get on a train and leave the CBD. The waiters spoke English, so it meant that everyone could ask questions or order, but I knew the ordering would fall to me. It always fell to me.

I found comfort in the efficiency of the waiters. The waitress greeted me in Mandarin and I responded in Cantonese, so she automatically switched to English. After seating us, she pressed on her radio set and informed the rest of the wait staff that I spoke Cantonese, took one look at Mike and brought over English menus.

'What just happened there?'

'We speak different dialects, but there's probably a few staff members here who speak Canto so they'll speak to me in Canto. English menus, 'cause, well, none of us can read in Chinese.' I spent six years of weekends at Chinese school learning Mandarin and all I can do is count, tell the time, ask for the toilet and tell people I like playing badminton (a lie, but a great way to start a conversation that I cannot carry).

Baby Chef, Shiteater and Camilla arrived together, clearly after a few drinks and with a bag full of wine bottles.

'I rang and they said they were BYO,' said Camilla, dumping five bottles on the table. She was finally putting her wine knowledge to use. Camilla was a recent hire to the wine team at The Restaurant, but she was very vocal about how much she hated it because the people who dined there weren't interested in wine that wasn't cheap.

'Sorry we're late, we didn't know what the booking was under,' said Shiteater through his red-wine-stained lips.

'All good. So, I had a quick flick through the menu. Is there anything you don't eat?'

'I'm not crazy about tofu,' said Shiteater.

'Too bad, I am going to change your mind.' I ordered a couple of baskets of the restaurant's specialty soup dumplings, which had just started popping up around the city, spring onion pancakes, fish head soup, braised pork belly with preserved vegetable, mapo tofu (I was gambling because this wasn't a Sichuan restaurant, but every region has its own interpretation of the dish), stir-fried snow pea sprouts and rice, lots of rice. Like a tour guide, I explained to everyone how to eat the soup dumplings, and warned them not to add any bloody soy sauce to their food.

'I will soy tax you, I swear. Don't soy me, bro.'

'Not even the dumplings?'

'Especially not the dumplings. You're meant to taste the meat and the broth. Fresh ginger and vinegar. Don't act like a tourist.'

'You know what, Jess, you're right about this tofu,' said

Shiteater, using his chopsticks to point to the dish.

'That's 'cause we don't use tofu as a meat substitute. It's an ingredient in its own right. It's there for its sweet, subtle flavour, as relief from fermented pastes and chilli sauces, and to complement the meat. No soy crimes.' It was an entry-level mapo tofu. This version was sweeter than it should have been, with the sauce-to-tofu ratio a little off and the heat dialled down to a friendly tickle. Just like my grandfather, I was not very good at gambling.

'I have news,' said Mike, setting down his chopsticks and taking a sip of wine. 'I quit. I got into post-grad law.'

'I also have news,' said Baby Chef. 'I also quit. I'm moving regional and working in an awesome restaurant.'

'And I quit, too,' said Camilla. 'I took a rep gig.'

We all looked at Shiteater. 'Chill out. I'm happy where I am.'

'Three out of four isn't bad,' I said. We cheered, drank and ate. Even though the restaurant was designed to appeal to a broader (read: whiter) audience, it didn't lack in the noise, conviviality, or vulgar-service departments. To me, it was comforting, because it meant the restaurant stood behind its product. After going around the country eating in wine bars with over-attentive service, surrounded by expensive furniture, it felt like each touchpoint of luxury was an apology to set up for the mediocre food. *Sure, the natural oysters were warm and dried out from being left under the heat lamps for too long, the cheese was fridge-cold and the accompaniments were stale, but we are drinking out of crystal Zalto glassware, and how nice was the waiter?* Fuck that. I'd rather have someone spit in my face and throw a basket of meticulously pleated, thin-skinned, collagen-filled soup dumplings at me with a sneer. If I feel like I'm in your way and you want me to get out as soon as you can, and I still want to come back to eat, you're a restaurant that does pretty fucking good food. I can buy my own Zalto glassware, open oysters and let cheese come up to temperature in my own home, but I don't have the time, space or skills to just bust out a basket of xiao long bao, or to three-step braise some pork belly on my two-burner induction stove.

'Oh shit, everyone quiet and don't draw attention to yourselves,' said Mike. He usually reserved this line for women he had slept with and untangled himself from in a messy manner. But it was all messy because these women wanted to start a life with Mike and, at least these days, he was more interested in opening a textbook. I glanced up quickly and saw that it was a try-hard, know-nothing, for-the-clicks, self-proclaimed food writer who'd recently met Mike at the bar and kept coming back to bother him, hoping he would ask her out on a date. I fucked up. She locked eyes with me.

'Now I know why you quit,' I said under my breath.

'Hi,' she said, standing there waiting for us to strike up a conversation with her. Baby Chef, Camilla and Shiteater just stared at her while they continued to chew on their food. She looked down at our table, 'Oh, what's that?'

'Pork,' I said.

'Is it good?'

'It depends on your palate, it's a really traditional dish.'

'Oh, good to know. I'm about to review this restaurant.' *No one cares.*

'What's the cut?'

'Belly.' *It is so obviously belly. My god, could you know even less about food?*

'Why isn't it crunchy?'

'Because *we*, the *Chinese*, value silky, gelatinous textures as much as we do crunchy.' I picked up a piece of the fish head out of the claypot and started sucking on its jawbone. 'It's all about balance and what else is on the table.' I took my tonal cues from the wait staff.

'Hi, Mike,' she said.

'Hi,' he said, looking away and picking at food.

I sucked the collagen from around the fish eye and spat out the hard, chalky centre, making sure it clinked loudly in the bottom of my bowl, 'Okay, bye,' I said to her.

Mike grabbed my knee to stop himself from laughing until she left.

'You're such a bitch, but that was so awkward,' said Camilla.

'What's new?'

A couple of weeks later, her online review came out raving about the pork belly dish. Mike sent me a screencap of the paragraph where she lifted my crumbs of knowledge about gelatinous textures. 'Tourist,' I responded.

I moved on from touring wine events after a year, sometime around the mid twenty-teens. Aside from feeling like I was living in someone else's perpetual teenage fantasy, there was a clear lack of boundaries between personal and professional lives that I didn't want to be tangled up in. I'd had enough drama in my life, and I refused to sort out the dramas that resulted from decisions I'd warned people not to make. I was sick of being the mediator. When people went on the road, they seemed to regress. They kept throwing around the phrase, 'What goes on tour, stays on tour' as if consequences didn't exist. But the consequences always came. Apple had just introduced 'the cloud' to its devices, and I saw a surprising number of people accidentally upload compromising photos to shared household devices because they didn't understand how the cloud worked. Idiots.

I paid the bills with copywriting work, which didn't give me the opportunity to entertain myself by putting on a mass-appeal basic bitch voice. Surprisingly, it pleased my clients. The more sarcastic and facetious I was, the more work I picked up. I wasn't sure if I hated myself for it, or loved fucking with everyone. Eventually, I grew bored of my own game.

I spent my down-time trawling job ads. I had already come to terms with the fact that I was a wage slave, but I was hoping there would be more to life than this. A few wine writers forwarded me an ad for a bars editor gig at a magazine, and it was the only thing that looked mildly interesting. I had to consult Mike. We decided to visit The Greek at work because he wanted us to taste a cocktail he was working on.

'Porta!' Nugget deliberately alerted the rest of the restaurant to my arrival in his Choice Bro Italiano accent. It became a joke that the customers were in on. The venue was all dark and polish, tablecloths and penguin suits until I walked in.

'Sit your arse up at the bar,' said The Greek, while spiking a docket. 'Mike's coming, right?'

'Yeah. He's right behind me.'

The Greek grabbed a tin and started measuring out alcohol. 'Look, I know you'll probably think I'm a joke, but you've got to work to your crowd.' I looked around the room and gave him an understanding nod. 'It's a truffle Martini.'

'An earth poo Martini?'

'Don't be like that. I infused all these white truffle ends from all our truffle dishes into this super high-end vodka,' (my copywriting spider senses started tingling). 'Serve it dry martini–style, and with a local black-truffled chocolate truffle on the side.'

'What an amazing gimmick.'

'Oh, the crowd loves them. It's great for our numbers.'

'Porta,' Nugget yelled again.

Mike looked fantastically out of place among the suits and

ties. 'Hey, how's it going?' He leaned into the bar, resting on his forearm, and shook The Greek's hand.

'Yeah, good, good. You're just in time. Let me know what you think about this.' Instead of getting us to share one Martini, he poured us one each. 'Don't worry about it, it's stuff that would have been chucked and bonus stock.'

'This is an excellent gift,' said Mike. We clinked our glasses and took a sip.

'It tastes like a vodka martini with bits in it,' I said. 'I think the fact that it's cold just mutes the truffle altogether. I hope you're charging these fools a buttload for it.' The Greek winked in response and put two chocolate truffles in front of us.

'Well, you certainly smell the truffle in these.' The experience was lacklustre, but perfect for the style of the restaurant. It would be a total crowd-pleaser, and people would come in just for this. It was trendy, buzzy, wanky, boozy and filled with perceived indulgence. Genius. The drink would be this season's status symbol, like eating gold leaf for the sake of shitting gold. No one ordering this drink would ask what the point of it is. I imagined The Greek sleeping on his mountain of cash tips.

'So, what's up?' asked Mike.

'Bars editor. Do you think I should go for it?'

'A hundred per cent. I mean, look at us right now. You can clearly do it. You have the palate; you have the knowledge. You can definitely write.' I realised that asking my number-one cheerleader may have been a mistake. Mike thought I was the best at everything.

'I don't have a journalism degree.'

'So? Fuck them. These idiots might have journalism degrees, but they don't know fuck about shit. They're the kind of people who drink this tasteless truffle drink and bang on about the luxury. At least you say it like it is. Everyone goes to you about food and drink anyways, you might as well get paid to do it.'

'I guess.'

'And like that chick at dinner. She stole your line about pork belly. She probably didn't even order rice. Just go for it. The worst they could say is no.' As usual, he was right. 'So, what's going on with your hair? Are you growing it out?' Mike ruffled through my hair like he was looking for lice.

'I dunno. I was thinking about it, but it's annoying as hell.'

'I'm going to shave your head after this. We're going back to mine.'

Mike's apartment smelled like sex and antiperspirant. The only bathroom in his apartment was an en suite so I had to walk into the heart of the musk.

'Dude. Warning.'

'Well, I didn't know you'd look all polite and shit and I'd have to fix you up. I know I need to wash my sheets.'

I stood in front of Mike's bathroom mirror as he plugged in his electric shaver.

'What are you overthinking about now?' asked Mike.

'Same stuff,' I said. He turned the shaver on, looked at my eyes in the reflection of his mirror and said, 'Just. Do. It.' Then he shaved a chunk out of the middle of my head, laughing like a maniac. He took before, during and after photos of us making a mess in his bathroom and posted it to all his social media accounts (he was the sentimental one).

Men I didn't know left comments on the photos saying I shouldn't have shaved my head 'cause hair made me pretty.

'Unfriend. Yuck. Who wants to be pretty when you can be a babe?' said Mike.

I got the gig.

It was a part-time role that required full-time hours and had average pay. I subsidised it with copywriting and rationalised to myself that I had to pay my dues. At least my drinks would be free. The gig was all done from home, which surprised me. I had not worked in a magazine environment before and assumed I'd need to be shown how they did things in the office. The from-home part finally made sense when I rocked up for an induction and was met with four women crammed into a makeshift plywood room, overheated from bodies and electronics in the middle of winter.

'It's cosy,' said the editor. I wondered if that's how the real estate agent sold the space, which failed to meet the 2.7-metre ceiling height standard. 'If you need to use the loo, it's just through here.' She led me through a door made from a single piece of wood hammered onto a flimsy frame, and I stared into the bowels of a bathroom that appeared to have remained uncleaned since the site's previous tenant left. After scrutinising it for a few seconds, I realised it wasn't dirty, the water had just left oxidised stains all over the porcelain because the room had no insulation. It reminded me of the facilities near my year-twelve common room.

'There's a snack shelf here where we keep all our food, but the market is just down the street and there are tonnes of cafes around, so we normally just grab something from the area.' The shelf was more of a ledge, far enough from the bathroom to be considered sanitary. On it was a tin of Nescafe Blend 43, a tin of Milo and an open value-pack of Indomie Mi Goreng sitting above a sink and a discoloured electric kettle. It was exactly like my year-twelve common room.

It was simple on paper. Two reviews of new venues, three news stories and a feature story every week to go online, and supplement stories to fill up box-outs in the monthly hard-copy magazine. I don't know what city these women were living in, but even at its height, Melbourne was not opening 104 review-worthy bars every year. It was harder, still, because the magazine didn't publish negative reviews. It had to be 104 *good* new bars every year.

'Oh, it's just a guide. You don't *need* to do two, but we would prefer it. And then you have the bar guide to write on top of that.

It's a guide to a hundred venues. There are categories like Best Cocktail Bar, Best Party Bar, Best Bartender and whatnot, and you determine the winners.'

'So, how does that work when I'm also writing new bars up every week? I'd have to visit existing bars while I'm doing the new bars, right? Or are there are a few of us that put the guide together?'

'Oh, it won't be as complicated as that. Head Office in Sydney will give you the outline of it, but you get six weeks or so to write the guide.' Six weeks did not sound like enough time to write a full guide on part-time hours on top of weekly editorial commitments. I could see that my hope had lead me to make a stupid decision.

But, at least I wasn't being sexually harassed while carrying plates. I was paying my dues. I'd be sitting on my arse the entire time anyway. Drinking, writing, making observations, judging, tapping away. I'd survived hospitality, I could survive anything.

Because I didn't work there full time, I wasn't assigned a company email, even though I had the word 'editor' attached to my role. I had to use my personal email and try to convince industry contacts and publicists to give me relevant information so I could do my job. I was running around the city like an arsehole, but at least I had Mike by my side. He sat through many overdiluted old fashioneds, poorly executed speakeasys, unstrained martinis with microshards of ice, saccharine Tiki-style drinks and faulty as fuck natural wines. He even cut his lip on a chipped tumbler. But best of all (for me), he would finish off all the crappy bar snacks I ordered, because a requirement of a bar review was to comment on the food. Back in those days, bar food was an afterthought, and the best you could hope for were scabs of pre-cut charcuterie from the market that were dried out as minimally as possible, overhandled and laid down on a damp chopping board with mass-produced sponge bread and pickles. Something would always taste cross-contaminated with bar prep because some poor bartender had to put the plate together.

'You forget, I survived off this shit,' Mike would say. 'I treat it like jerky. I've developed a taste for dried-up salumi now.' Eventually, thankfully, restaurants started opening offshoot bars a few doors down from their main sites. When we shared a plate of deep-fried confit lamb ribs with chilli jam; oysters shucked to order; and twenty-dollar-a-tin Portuguese preserved fish, Mike rolled up his sleeves, flexed both his biceps and said, 'This is how you accumulate mass.'

Due to our limited resources, I would file my copy to an editor in Sydney who had nothing to do with the food section. The logic was that if he could understand what I was saying through all the booze and food jargon, it was fit for the general public. There was a precarious moment when I had to explain to him the difference between a drink being served up or on the rocks, but the experience made us both better writers and more tolerant people. I valued him as an editor because he forced me to get uncomfortable and stop using industry lingo. Much like a therapist, instead of telling me, he coaxed me into realising that the more easily you convey something, the better a writer you are. If you manage to passively educate someone along the way, then you've won. No ego, no jargon, no bullshit.

The fact-checking part of everything is what got me. When they first told me the articles got fact-checked, I imagined a team of fact-checkers sitting behind phones and calling people to ask if they said what I wrote, whether they prepared or served their products the way I described; that the ingredients I listed were correct; and that my perceived flavour profile was approximately correct, the way the formidable fact-checking department of the *New Yorker* would stress-test each of its articles. Instead, it was just me, calling up venues after the fact to check that everything I was writing was okay. I took photos of rooms, menus and drinks as evidence, but I still took everything owners said with a grain of salt. I knew through my industry experience that restaurants saying their eggs are organic don't know the difference between organic and free-range; those who claim they have a 'kitchen garden' give the impression that all their produce is from a tiny patch of earth, when in reality, they buy in eighty per cent of their perishables; and when you drink alcohol mixed out of crystal that has been siphoned off from branded bottles, they're not top-shelf spirits. The truth never came from the owners, but from the workers who processed, prepped and pre-batched everything. They were usually more than happy to throw their dodgy employers under the bus. When it came down to writing the bar guide, I couldn't afford to be hungover every day, so I would carry around an opaque drink bottle, pretend to drink from it and spit my cocktail into it after tasting. It kept my palate unmarred by drunkenness, and I also remembered details from each venue. I allowed myself thirty minutes at each bar before moving on, with an aim to hit seven to nine venues a night. I'd hide in the bathroom making notes, rinsing out my spittoon-in-disguise for the next venue. For a long time, every single social outing was dictated by my part-time role with no company email.

'You're no fun anymore,' Mike would say when I tucked him into bed. He'd be blotto from finishing off all my drinks. He was half-joking, but it was true. When I was handed a budget to pay for my drinking habit, I eventually lost my desire for alcohol. Succumbing to hope and diversifying my resume was killing my passions, one vice at a time.

11

I am not made for television. Not in the way that my appearance is so mangled that I only have a voice for radio, but because I am a non-conformist, fourth-wave feminist and I proudly don't fit into any heteronormative pigeonholes that are a requirement in prime-time broadcasting. Also, I don't care if I'm likeable.

I spent years learning to carry myself in a particular way so that if I don't know you, I don't appear threatening, but you know not to approach me unless you absolutely fucking have to. When my very good friend and hairdresser gave me a fringe for a change-up, I grew it out as quickly as I could because strangers began to stop me in the street to ask for directions.

Yet, for some reason, I was chased down through social media not once, not twice, but three times by a casting agent asking me to consider being a judge on a rebooted food show. The first time I said I wasn't interested, the casting agent asked to meet for coffee so she could explain the concept a bit better. The second time I said no, she said I should think about it. The third time, she said she wanted to send a camera-phone clip of me having a conversation with her so the producers could see if I fit with the rest of the judges.

I owned a television, but I was always unplugging it to use the power socket for something else. All my pop-culture references were over a decade old and were only kept fresh in my mind from rewatching shows I torrented and saved to an external hard drive. The only contemporary television I watched was *RuPaul's Drag Race* on SBS in the middle of the night when I wasn't drunk enough to fall asleep. So, when the casting agent told me that this food show wouldn't be like all the others, I had no idea what she meant.

'The contestants will be setting up real restaurants and serving real customers. It won't be a cooking competition format. You'll be able to speak to your experience,' she told me. 'There's another show being developed on another network that's a cooking competition, essentially trying to copy what is on every other network. We think there are too many in this genre. What we are bringing to the screen will be refreshing to the audience. It will be real.' I didn't have the heart to tell her that after working all day around food and drink, the last thing I wanted to watch were non-professionals doing my profession poorly, so I just nodded.

It was a nine-month process of the casting agent chipping away at me. During that time, Mike and I went to New York for another urban snow adventure, and we showed each other our versions of the city. Late one evening, as we sat with the kitchen crew from Daniel, ceremoniously eating Korean ramyun at the bar of Hanjan, Hooni said to me, 'If they're offering you the role of a judge, you should do it.' I looked around the room and saw a few K-Pop stars finishing off their meals and taking selfies. Due to Hooni's role as a judge on Korean *MasterChef*, he became huge in Korea while maintaining his anonymity in New York. 'I wouldn't recommend being a contestant,' he said. I'd learn what he meant by that over the next year, but my three solid noes somehow turned into a very tentative yes.

As soon as I signed the contract, the executive producer called me to introduce herself. I was trying not to get run over while jaywalking aggressively to the site of a wine bar that I was months away from opening. Mike kept making jokes about me dying at twenty-seven, so I was uneccesarily anxious when crossing the street. I'd never wanted to open my own venue, but the landlord who would become by business partner offered me a deal I couldn't refuse, and I was due for a challenge. If traffic wasn't going to kill me, it would be the bar.

'I'm so glad we signed you up – we wanted you from the very beginning,' she said over the phone.

'Great.' I had no idea how to respond to that but said 'great' to seem more personable.

'I was just calling to get a sense of your style because I think we should get you in touch with our stylist as soon as possible. We are cutting it a bit fine, here.' I ran across two lanes and waited for the traffic to pass in the middle of the road at a tram stop.

'Well, I'm short, muscular and broad. I have coathanger shoulders, huge quads from Muay Thai, a short torso and I'm built like a brick because I was on a shitload of steroids as a kid for my eczema and asthma. Good luck to her,' I said, standing on a traffic island while scanning left and right.

'You make yourself sound like a monster.'

'Not at all. I am just very aware of my proportions because I have been dressing myself for my entire life. I am not of European descent, so I don't fit into standard Australian sizing. I'm just stating facts, they're not positive or negative attributes. Bodies are different.'

'That's refreshing. I'll pass on your number, is that okay?'

'Go ahead.' I made it onto a footpath.

Despite mostly dressing for function, my wardrobe was surprisingly stacked. Basically, if it was a bedsheet with sleeves, I was all about it. My closet was full of draped, loose-fitting, structural garments from Yamamoto, Mason Margiela, Comme des Garcons, Acne, Alpha60 and Claude Maus, and I didn't necessarily shop from the women's section. If you included my underwear, my clothes were a forty-sixty split of female to male categorised clothing. I didn't believe in gendered clothing. The less of my body and its shape that you could see, the better.

'You can't wear black on the show. Another judge said that's his colour,' said Executive Producer.

'What is he, Cadbury trying to own purple? He's not even from Melbourne.' Executive Producer chuckled and explained to me that since he was the big-name mainstream chef on the panel, whatever he wanted, he would get.

'Don't stress. Stylist can arrange a time to come around and look at your clothes. She can build a wardrobe for you from there. Thankfully, we have a good budget, which isn't normal for the first year of a show.'

Stylist was Sydney-based and flew in with ten bags of clothes. She was staying in a hotel a few blocks from my apartment and brought options to show me after we had a brief phone call about what labels I wore and what size I was. She and Executive Producer came to my apartment and tore through my closet, getting me to try on almost everything I owned so they could see for themselves what worked.

'I can't believe you own this,' Stylist said, holding up my black rubber Gareth Pugh dress. 'What's that smell?'

'Rubber cleaner. You can't exactly put it through the wash.' I kept taking photos of their confused faces and sending them to Mike. He sent voice messages in return which I knew without having to play them were just clips of him laughing.

'Oh, this is nice.' Stylist yanked a few knits out of my drawer that were Mike's. I wore so much oversized clothing that Mike and I could basically swap wardrobes, and we regularly changed at each other's apartments. 'Oh, they're huge. And black.' She folded them up and put them back. I played dress-ups for an hour or so and Stylist picked a few main items of clothing that she would use as the base for a lot of the show's outfits. There was only one piece of clothing that wasn't black, and it was my mother's red and white, short-sleeved silk shirt from her Cathay Pacific uniform thirty years ago.

'Just letting you know, that shirt doesn't fit the day after strength and conditioning or kettlebell classes.'

'Why?'

''Cause my arms fill with blood and then the buttons on the cuffs don't close around my biceps. I can force them closed but then it looks like you're trying to squeeze raw sausage out of the casing.' Stylist smiled and made a note. I already liked how she didn't discourage me from living my life just to fit into clothes that would make her job easier.

'Do you mind if I send you a few photos of clothing options? Then I can whittle it down. I'm here for a few days. Just message me your thoughts and we can meet up at my room and you can try on some stuff.'

I learned that on productions like these, everyone involved in the project freelanced. They were all free, unencumbered and travelled around for their jobs. What a life. Even though I had no intentions of having my new wine bar for life, the job of opening it, setting it up, and having it run and make money before I offloaded it to someone willing to pay me what it was worth was a two to three-year project. Giving it your all for three months and then changing gears sounded much more sustainable. From what Stylist told me, there was very little job insecurity because the industry was so small, everyone knew what you did, and you lined up new work before your current job was over. The ten bags she'd carried into the state weren't all for me. She was working a few gigs at once.

Stylist left, but Executive Producer stuck around to talk to me about timelines. We sat in my kitchen with the blinds still pulled down, the tryptic from the Dirty Playground launch three years ago looming over us.

'Are you comfortable filming or having photos taken inside your apartment? I'm just asking in case some media request it.'

'It will probably be filled with boxes and samples soon, so it's not ideal. Plus, I don't think the art is particularly mainstream.' Executive Producer stared at the gaping mouths and horrific faces taking up the wall and made some notes.

'We can work it out. So, it will probably be two to three days of filming for the next twelve weeks and travel to a different state every week after we determine the contestants. You'll have a bit of media to do for us as part of your contract outside of that. Are you going to keep growing your hair?' She spoke in dot points.

'I haven't really thought about it.' I was mushrooming and was well overdue a haircut.

'I've googled you and have seen that you shave your head quite a bit. Don't shave your head.'

'Um, okay.'

'What's your make-up situation like?'

'I don't have a make-up situation. I wear eyeliner if I'm hungover to hide the fact that I'm hungover.' Even that was a recent development.

'Do you know how to put on make-up?'

'Definitely not. I've always been too lazy for that.' Executive Producer made more notes.

'I'll make sure there's someone to do your face in every city. Are you allergic to any make-up?'

'I don't know. I have eczema so I've never bothered to try.' More notes.

'So, we are thinking of shooting an intro clip next week sometime and then we will be filming the first few days in Adelaide. What's your schedule like next week? Can you do Monday?'

'How long will the shoot take?'

'A few hours. Make-up, staging, we'll get a few scenes on location. What's the state of the bar at the moment?'

'It's a brick room with a hole in it.' Notes.

'I'll send you a schedule and we can be in touch. I won't be here for the intro clip, but I'll be in Adelaide. We'll be on the same flight.'

'Great.'

Executive Producer handed me a stack of cab charges. 'For your travel. Keep track of any expenses and we'll reimburse you.' What a luxury. In the past, I'd always have to chase and justify my reimbursements. Was this what making it felt like?

When I turned up to Stylist's hotel room, she had a whole queen-sized bed covered in clothes with their tags still attached for me to say yes or no to. I was apologetically wearing a layer of dust over my utilitarian uniform from doing a walk-through with the builders. She told me not to worry and held up a bright-pink polyester dress.

The dress stirred up a bunch of feelings I had forgotten about. It made me think of my family telling me to be more like a girl when I was growing up. They'd force me into flowery dresses and frilly socks and get me to play with dolls. I wasn't interested. I wanted to pour salt on snails in the garden, deep-fry fish and help my dad wash his car in shorts and a singlet. Every time I was told no, I told them I hated being a girl and said I should have been born a boy. How dare they do this to me? Around the same time, my dad sat me down and explained to me that my aunty was now an uncle, and to not make the mistake of calling him aunty anymore. I asked him why he got to be a boy and wear singlets and I couldn't. My dad just told me that was the way it was. That was the end of the conversation. Culturally, I knew I wasn't allowed to ask any more questions, and this was the way life was going to be. It wasn't fair. I hated my reflection and avoided mirrors until I was a teenager. By then, even though I was unhappy in my body, I knew being a boy wouldn't make me happier. I hated being a girl, but being a boy wouldn't give me inner peace. Instead, I looked at my body like a meat sock for my brain, and I was able to manage the misery around my physicality. I never saw who I was reflected back at me until I cut all my hair off and gave myself permission to reject binary definitions.

I studied the dress. 'I don't know about that,' I said.

'Just try it on. I think you'll look great, especially with your skin tone.' I squirmed around in it and Stylist took a photo and sent it to Executive Producer. Her phone chimed almost immediately, and she said, 'You're off the hook. We can't mic you up properly in that.' Thank fuck. I felt like I was being suffocated in someone else's identity.

There was a procession of form-fitting, pastel-coloured, low-cut graments and open-toed shoes being exhibited to me. I could see Stylist trying to hide the fact that she was briefed for a different person altogether. Somehow, between our phone call and when she got on the plane, I was going to transform into a youthful, carefree, colourful, non-threatening femme.

We agonisingly, but politely, compromised on whites, greens and blues.

'I'll think of it like a costume,' I said, trying to console Stylist and convince myself.

The day of the intro shoot, I sat in a chair with a make-up artist discussing my problematic skin.

'But you have great skin,' she said.

'That's 'cause I don't aggravate it by putting shit all over it.'

'Make-up's come a long way. I think your skin would be fine with water-based.' Were we talking lubricants or make-up? Make-up Artist unzipped a luggage bag I could fit in packed with palettes, brushes and other modern torture devices I didn't know the names of. She mixed a bunch of paint together to match my skin tone, put it in a gun and sprayed it on my face.

'Are you spray painting my skin the colour of my skin?'

'Yeah, it's so you don't show up shiny on camera. So, what's your look?'

'My look?'

'You know, glam, natural, dramatic?'

'Sunscreen?'

She laughed. 'How about I try something and see what production think of it?'

'Sure.' I had no idea what I was in for. After having my eyes closed for half an hour and missing my own teen coming-of-age transformation montage, I saw a reflection. It wasn't me. It was bronzed, buffed, blushed, glossed, curled and perfect for general mass-consumption, but it wasn't me. It was the kind of reflection I couldn't bear to look at as a child. I didn't want to hurt Make-up Artist's feelings, so I had to swallow my distress. I clenched my fists so hard that I managed to dig half-moon marks from my meticulously clipped nails into my palms.

The thing that no one had ever told me about make-up is that it is very heavy on your skin. I couldn't breathe. The mascara on my crimped eyelashes weighed my eyelids down. I felt like I was in a gender re-education camp and each stroke of colour was like a drip of water on my forehead. I tried not to freak out at how smothered I felt and deployed a tactic I'd learned in therapy. I started counting the number of things around the room. Five people, three water glasses, six chairs, twenty-one steps, three windows, one door.

'Are you okay?' asked Make-up Artist.

'It's just a bit hot.' I stood up and walked towards a window.

'That's actually very good lighting. I'll just take a photo of you for production and see what they think.' I grabbed a glass of water and started chugging it. 'Gorgeous. Beautiful. They love it.'

I remember wanting to be a lot of things when I grew up, but gorgeous was not one of them. I wanted to be smart, brilliant, hard-working, happy, resilient. I focused on the resilient. *It's just make-up. It's just a costume. It's not who I am.* I could get through this.

Twelve indoor plants. Two sinks. Six phones. Two mirrors. One hideous rug.

After the shoot wrapped, I went straight to a meeting with the chef of the wine bar to drill down on the concept of the menu.

'What's with the face?'

'Don't even. I can't.'

'Do you want me to hose it off?'

'I'll need it. Fuck. I need to buy make-up remover.' This interaction was the opposite of ones I'd had with chefs in the early years of my career. Working in Docs always led the back-of-house crew to ask me if I was a lesbian. How the times had changed.

Chef had a reputation of being a rough old English geezer. There were rumours of prison, the breaking of bones and all kinds of violence, but I only saw a trained palate, unfussy food and excellent sauce work. We understood each other. 'You'll be okay,' he said comfortingly. 'You're a pain in my arse however you look.' He caused my first unprompted smile of the day.

'They're fucking with my gender expression,' I whinged to Mike, purposely rubbing layers of face all over his t-shirt. 'You know why women have no time for anyone's shit?'

'Why?'

''Cause society says they have to wear pancake face all the fucking time.'

He looked down at his clothes. 'We need to scrub.'

We perched over the sink in my bathroom, splashing a newly purchased bottle of thirty-dollar micellar water onto cotton pads and soaking my face off with it. Mike kept rubbing circles across my skin, mixing the pinks with the yellows, the blacks and the browns, and with each rinse, the layers would fade a little. Three washes later, I could breathe again. I dried my face on a towel and it still picked up traces of paint.

'You need to be nicer to the women who fall in love with you,' I said. 'They voluntarily put this crap on their face every time they see you. It's expensive and time-consuming. Even if you pay for their meals and drinks, I bet they're still cash-negative from getting ready.'

'I don't ask them to wear make-up. And fuck you, I am nice. Why else do you think they're in love with me?'

'But you meet them with it on so that's the face they're comfortable showing you. Either way, society is fucked.' I threw one of my t-shirts at Mike and he handed me his powder-covered one to put through the wash.

'How many more times do you have to do this?'

'Exactly too many more times.'

'Why are they making you look like such a hardcore female?'

'Probably because I'm the only one with a vagina.' I meant that as a joke, but I was right. I was seated next to Executive Producer on the flight to Adelaide and she briefed me on everyone else who had been cast on the panel. I either knew them already or knew of them from working in the industry.

It became obvious during the briefing session that I was the only one in the room under thirty, with zero divorces behind me, who was not a male and whose ancestors originated from an entirely different continent. Just by standing in the room, I was ticking a tonne of diversity boxes.

We were all assigned specialties. We were 'experts'. Our categories were chef, food reviewer, front of house and social media. It was an incredibly simplified way to break down the hospitality ecosystem to a mainstream audience, but this was prime time. No one really wants to know how the sausage gets stuffed. *It won't be like other food shows.*

It was exactly like other food shows.

The show was adamant on selling me as the social media expert even though I had done a lot more than that in my career, and it wasn't lost on me that making a young Asian person the internet geek was a very convenient casting choice. *Please, shower me with more stereotypes. Martial arts, piano, maths? I can do it all!* Hilariously, it was the older white men in the room who were addicted to their infinite scrolls. I'd made a point of keeping the internet separate from my actual life, so the only notifications I had on my phone were text messages and calls. I relished watching grown men who limited their own spawns' screen time having a Pavlovian response to a hand-held ding.

We were all virgins to the process. Sure, we all may have been interviewed before or sat on panels, but we had no idea how television on this scale was made. The show was supported by sponsors, so our filming obligations were tied to them. Even though we didn't need to be on set until 10 or 11am, I had a call time of 4.30 or 5am to get my face made up. I was always the first cab off the rank because I was the female, and according to unwritten television law, no man should get his make-up applied before a woman because she will take the longest. So I'd always be standing around for two hours after my dead-straight Asian hair had been ironed and my face had been pancaked. Because I'm from Melbourne, I refused to drink hotel coffee, so I brought beans, a grinder and a V60 with me and made everyone coffee to fill in the time.

For the first day of filming, I was assigned to wear a leather dress. I squeezed into it and thought that it was cold, but fine. I'd get used to it. Then the sound department said they had to mic me up and we were met with coverage issues. I ended up with a mic pack strapped to my inner thigh, a pack stuck to my spine that was forcibly zipped over, and a microphone taped to my chest. *This is how the sausage gets stuffed. I am the sausage.* The men all hid their electronics in jacket pockets. *My kingdom for a jacket or a pocket.*

One of the sponsors was a car brand, so the first hours of shooting involved us being driven around in circles with cameras in our faces for two seconds of usable content. In theory, this is an easy shot, but I have motion sickness. I held up a lot of scenes having to get out, stand up and gasp for air.

When it got down to determining the contestants, the crew who prepared us for the process by improvising pitches were a lot more dynamic, well-spoken and attractive than the lot of us. In our break, I asked one of the crew who presented why he wasn't on the other side of the camera. He handed me a blanket to keep me warm and said, 'I'd rather be the puppet master than the puppet.' I was so restricted in my clothing that it took three throws for me to get the blanket all the way around. As I struggled to keep my dignity intact, I realised I was talking to the smartest person in the room.

Then, my nipples became a problem. Or to be more accurate, they were *perceived* to be a problem. There was a seam on either side of the front panel of the dress that was designed to make room for the breasts I do not have. The end of each seam finished where my nipples would logically line up under the dress, so Stylist was called into emergency action to make sure it wasn't so cold that my areolas were visible through a sheet of dead cow. After giving me heat packs to warm my hands under the table, sticking them inside my shoes and making me undress so she could tape down my nipples that were already covered with a bra, it was confirmed that it was just the stitching of the dress. We had shot half the episode with me in the dress already, so for continuity's sake, everyone and my taped-up tits powered through to the end.

Then, there were photos.

We were required to have profile shots done for the show's site. The men all stood tall with their shoulders back, emphasising their good sides. Classic man poses with hands in pockets, behind their backs, one over the other, crossed over their chests. I was useless. I hated being photographed and pulled pained, awkward faces as soon as I was aware a camera was on me. It was uncontrollable. As a twenty-something of the internet age, I was uncommonly averse to having my photograph taken. I strongly believe that the more photos you take of yourself, the more narcissistic, insecure and unhinged you are. What are all these photos for? Are you going to forget what you look like? Mike was the only person who had photos of me, and most of the time I was swearing at him for taking a photo of me in the first place. I had no idea how to take a photo without either a prop (Mike) or spitting a profanity (at Mike).

'Relax,' said the photographer. All I could feel were the hard corners of a mic pack digging into my back, forcing my spine to curve forward.

'What? You mean I don't look relaxed?' I couldn't help screwing my face up and pulling my head into my neck like a startled turtle. I was intensely aware that my face was so scrunched into itself that I looked like that over-steamed dumpling stuck to the edge of the bamboo basket that everyone avoided at yum cha. I'd settle for looking like the matchmaker from Mulan if this whole process could be over and done with.

We both did the best we could, and when the photographer said he got the shot, I let myself go. He took one more photograph. I'm fairly certain that's the photo production chose.

The process got a bit easier after every episode we filmed. I was no longer bothered by having my face suffocated while my body froze in synthetic drapery. Executive Producer even openly discussed the failings of certain teams and asked me to poke and prod at their weak points. It was just a job.

'Are you non-stop filming all day?' Mike asked me.

'It's more of a "hurry up and wait", thing. Oh my god, you have to get up at four to get into a cab so you can get on the red-eye and fly to whatever state you're meant to be in and then get another cab to meet the hair and make-up artist. Hurry, hurry, hurry and wait for a few hours. Shit, quick, get in the car so we can make you car sick for an hour. And wait until everyone's here. Oh, shit, it's raining. Just sit in the car and wait. But fuck, come on, let's film your piece to camera right now, outside. The radar says it isn't going to be wet for five minutes, and quickly, go back inside and wait. Let's film you walking twenty-five times just to make sure we have the shot. Wait here. Keep waiting. On and on until the day is over. You're booked for the whole day but do about an hour's worth of real work. It makes me anxious because I'm used to needing everything done by yesterday.'

'It sounds ... boring.'

'Yeah, it is. It's an experience. I didn't know and now I know. By the way, I need an eating partner for the Melbourne restaurant. Wanna be naughty on TV?'

'What do I have to do?'

'Look pretty and eat.'

Episodes started airing. Unsurprisingly, the public hated me, but I was too busy setting up the bar to care. The people in my life didn't watch television because they were too busy doing their jobs, so it had no effect on me.

According to the peanut gallery, I was not feminine enough, not nice enough, not encouraging enough, not smiley enough, not thin enough, not pretty enough, not hot enough, not experienced enough, not Asian enough, not Australian enough, just not enough of anything, really. Executive Producer and the men on the panel all messaged with screencaps of tweets calling me a bitch or a cunt asking if I was okay. I told them all I was used to being called worse things. It's what happens when you're a woman who doesn't blindly praise people for their poor efforts. I was the one doing my job properly, they weren't. The viewers were expecting a smiling Hello Kitty and instead they got a Tiger Mum. It was a primetime crime, and viewers wanted me thrown in television jail. One of the other experts suggested that I smile more.

It reminded me of being in grade three music class. My music teacher was in awe of the fact that I was playing at a grade five AMEB level, sightreading sheet music and sitting music theory exams alongside VCA students while every other kid was sticking a recorder up their nose. But he still told me that the other kids would be nicer to me if I smiled. He even went as far as to tell me that I was prettier when I smiled, which made me not want to smile at all. Besides, what kind of crazed maniac could smile while trying not to fuck up Bach with their prepubescent hands?

'It's just my face,' I'd say.

Behind the scenes, I caused a lot of heated discussion. Aside from having to retape pieces to camera because I used language deemed too complex for their target audience, I also made comments that required forty-eight hours of debate. For instance, there were incredibly inexperienced contestants who tried to work in low-cut tops and heels, and I brought up the fact that they were going to be in a lot of pain and risk injury because they were too busy performing gender instead of performing their roles. After much discussion, my critique was ultimately cut.

I was also receiving very inappropriate messages from someone in the production. It was no secret. This person spoke sleazily to me in front of the crew as if no one else was in the room and always touched me in the no-no space. He didn't even bother to censor himself when my mic was turned on, and there was an engineer on the other end who could hear everything he was saying to me. There were also highly incriminating emails that copied in other people when he accidentally pressed 'reply all'. Still, he was untouchable.

I received more screencaps asking if I was okay. Like any other 26-year-old woman in a field with no experience and no power, I just ignored it. If hospitality had taught me anything, it's that if you work hard enough and bring as little attention to the harassment as possible, the harasser will get bored and move on. Essentially, the tactic is to defuse the attention by playing dumb. A couple of the experts informed Executive Producer just in case she was unaware, and she responded saying that I was a capable woman who could handle myself, and if I needed help, I would ask.

I was strategically separated from this person so we were no longer physically in the same place at the same time, which was lucky for them because I was due to film my dinner with Mike.

Inevitably, during our dinner we were shooshed, hushed, paused and censored. We were just being us, which was too much for a PG-13, 7pm program. Feedback from Executive Producer was that it was the episode that the public grew to like me because I gave positive feedback (that was rightly earned) and I smiled a lot. I was forwarded comments that said I was pretty and Mike was a hunk. God, I hated people. Who even used the word hunk?

The show predictably bombed. While it was 'not like every other food show on television', it really, really was. I was relieved that it wasn't being renewed. Aside from feeling like it was in the way of all the real work that I wanted to do, it made me realise that I hated being seen.

After not speaking to my mother for over a decade, except at family funerals, I received many lengthy emails from her criticising the way I looked, telling me to not spend money on make-up and new clothes, telling me to smile more and be nice, along with links to articles breaking down television ratings, suggestions on how to make myself more likeable and how the show could be edited better. It was bizarre behaviour but not out of character for her.

Even a trip to buy dishwashing tablets involved strangers coming up to me and saying, 'You know, you're actually a really nice person.' Tyre-kickers would visit the wine bar, order the cheapest glass on the menu after making me describe the entire list and say, 'You actually know what you're talking about.'

Being a well-recognised, one-dimensional, talking head is a dream for some, but it is not for me.

I am not made for television.

12

One morning, I woke up to two messages. One was from Mike's brother, and the other was from his mother. My mouth dried up, my breath shortened, my heart pounded so loudly in my chest I could feel my pulse in my ears, and I wanted to throw up. Without opening the messages, I knew.

Mike died from suicide.

Over the years, our friendship had evolved from heavy drinking and late nights to bouts of sobriety and supporting each other through depressive episodes. We'd see each other's sadness smothering each other before we knew it ourselves. Mike would always cancel our plans to do nothing, citing study as a priority, and I would always ask him if we had a choice between being stupid and happy or being smart and sad, which option he would go with. (He always chose smart and sad because he said I hated stupid people and he couldn't imagine his life without me.) There was always a starting point of irreversible sorrow.

We lived in each other's pockets. We were each other's lifelines, back-up, support networks and wallets. If Mike had a few drinks and couldn't thumb through his money properly but still wanted to shout me, he would stick his arms up in the air as a signal for me to dive in his pockets, pull his cash out on the table, tip appropriately, and return his change to his hip. Then, he'd say, 'Straighten me out,' to signal that I should line up the layers under his jacket. If we split up to go home, we'd text to let each other know we'd gotten home safe, and inevitably watch the same show at the same time in our apartments. His would be the last text I received before falling asleep. When he got a dog, his was also the first text I woke up to, synching my consciousness with his pet's morning dump.

The night before, I hadn't received a text from Mike as I was falling asleep. He hadn't even respond to my last text, which was my way of checking in on him if I hadn't heard from him in a few hours. He was finishing his papers for his last semester of law and was also putting together course work for a subject his lecturer was pushing him to teach on cryptocurrency and other things I didn't understand, so he'd implemented black-out hours where he put his phone on airplane mode to charge through work uninterrupted. Occasionally, he'd fall asleep and forget to turn airplane mode off, and in moments of depression, I'd work myself into an anxious fit and pass out from exhaustion, only to wake up to an apology.

That morning, the apology I received was from Mike's brother, in a whisper. I called his mother and she asked me to tell all his friends what had happened because she didn't know where to start. The truth was, I didn't either. We'd become so insular in our old age.

Mike had deactivated all his social media accounts a year before his death. He hated all the time he spent scrolling through everyone's nothing updates.

'But screencap funny shit for me,' he said. Aside from memes and clips from *It's Always Sunny in Philadelphia*, he was partial to a good hate-follow. He bowed out of social media because he said it was the easiest way to cut toxic people out of his life. An unfortunate side-effect of working in hospitality for so long is being friends with people who don't know how to stop drinking and taking drugs like they're still twenty. It's fine for some, but when you have underlying sadness and volatile mental health, it's best to separate yourself from the scene altogether because the peer pressure is relentless, and certain nights out cracked Mike wide open.

I hadn't spoken to a lot of people for months. I was also depressed, recovering from trauma, and trying to get through the day without a meltdown. I made an inventory of all the people Mike and I knew in common and started calling, ticking off names and making notes like I was working an invites list in PR mode.

The reactions from our friends ranged from shock (a gasp, a sorry and a hang up), to sadness (immediate crying), to selfishness ('I can't believe this is happening to me'), to grief leeching (offers of support followed by invasive questions surrounding Mike's death) and anger ('You know, he's always been a selfish little shit'). It made me realise Mike made the right choice in wiping his social media accounts. Even though I knew Mike was gone, my natural reaction after every phone call was to text him about each interaction. Stopping myself made my chest tighten each time.

I went to meet Mike's brother the next day. His parents had just gotten into Melbourne from Mildura but couldn't bring themselves to go into his apartment. I rang the doorbell and his brother opened the door. It had been a few years since we had seen each other, and he hugged me before we said anything. He smelled like Mike. It wasn't his cologne; it was his skin. Their grief had the same scent. It was the smell that Mike would have after every heartbreak, failure or shit day. It was the smell he would suffocate me with when he needed a hug.

'Where's Sosu?' I wasn't used to entering Mike's apartment without his dog running up to me and attacking my laces.

'Mum and Dad have her at the neighbour's.' I imagined Mike's French bulldog scratching at the door for her morning walk while Mike was lifeless in the other room. Since Mike had got Sosu and broken up with his bartending persona, he'd flipped his schedule so he woke up at 5.30am to walk his dog with his neighbour and went to bed at 9.30pm. It was hard for me to register that Mike wasn't there. We had the keys to each other's apartments, and I was used to letting myself in while he was at uni to drop off food I'd cooked for him. His apartment had the same musty, unventilated smell it always had. His shoes were stinking up the hallway, the bathroom was perpetually damp, bowls were crusty with food and soaking in the kitchen sink.

Mike had printed out a passport renewal form and left it by the front door. We'd travelled together for his thirtieth birthday and talked about going overseas again. I could see that he'd filled out the form and dated it a few days ago, and all he needed was a new passport photo.

'Thanks for coming. I don't know what we are going to do with all his stuff yet. We need to find a few things, but do you want to take something to remember him by?'

'What do you need to find? Need some help?'

'We've got most of the important documents, we know his phone provider and everything. Mum really wanted his scarf and that quartz necklace he wore all the time. I can't find it.'

'Should we start in his room?'

'Let me wedge the door open. I just can't have it closed.' That was where he'd found him.

We found Mike's scarf on his coat stand, along with every single jacket he'd asked me to approve before he purchased it. Mike's bed was unmade, his pillows covered in skin particles from his beard. Every time the seasons changed, he'd have to lather his face up in beard oil because the sudden shift in temperature would dry out his skin.

'Do you want to go through his bed or his laundry?' I asked.

'Am I going to find some kinky shit if I choose his bed?'

'You might find sweaty, old clothes, but if you want to be safe, I can do both.' In the past, a few of his exes had described his penis to me as beautiful. He'd told me stories of sexual mishaps and the pain of getting a Prince Albert redone through scar tissue, but when we slept together, we always shared the bed as brother and sister.

I dug through Mike's dirty laundry, which was extra musky because he'd just taken up Brazilian Jiu Jitsu with one of my old trainers and his gis were marinating in a mixture of socks, jocks and singlets. I checked though every pocket from his jackets and had to push away memories attached to each item of clothing. It wasn't the time to get emotional. I found old receipts, hankies, coins, but no quartz necklace.

'I think we should call up the martial arts school and the Carlton Baths to see if it's in lost property. We also need to cancel his memberships.' A few days before, Mike had texted me about a man swimming at the Carlton Baths who looked just like Danny DeVito and it had made his morning. That was until he was in the changerooms with all the seniors who possessed unshakeable body confidence – even after pruning up their floppy bits for the better part of an hour.

'Do you have their numbers?'

'I'll text one of the trainers at the gym. We can just google the baths.'

'Let's go to the kitchen to do this. I can't be in this room anymore,' said Mike's brother.

We passed three copies of *The Art of War* on the way to the kitchen, including one that sat on top of the toilet cistern. Mike was committed to the long game. He had a lot of plans. One was to laud his power over someone who'd fucked him over in the past, which was still a few years away from happening. Another was to buy a house, and for us live together when we were both old and widowed. We'd sit on a porch in rocking chairs with shotguns over our laps, talking shit and yelling at youths to fuck off, managed by our full-time, live-in carers. In the future, we were rich.

Mike's brother offered me water after I pointed at the cupboard he kept his glasses in, and I remembered how we'd almost bought a two-bedder to live in together when this project was being sold off the plan. As Mike's brother was on the phone to the baths, I looked around the room. Bottles of mezcal he'd brought back from California, matchbooks he'd collected from venues he used to work at, artworks he'd bought off our Dirty Playground artists, containers of spring water he'd driven out to the country to collect, beeswax wraps his mother had made for him to pass on to me, the dumbells he had in front of his couch so he could work on his glamour muscles while watching television. Knowing Mike wasn't coming home made his apartment feel like a shrine. I was standing in a room full of last times. This was the end of the story.

'Do you know his passwords?' Mike's brother needed to get into his accounts to disconnect everything.

'Not anymore. He changed them regularly.' Over the past year, Mike had grown increasingly paranoid of people gaining access to all his personal information. He'd been falling into information holes about the dark web as he researched for his course. He changed his passwords more than he changed his underwear.

We sat down for a breather opposite each other in the cramped dining space. There were a thousand things to discuss, but we didn't know where to start. I looked around and realised we were sitting in a deceased estate. Mike had gone from being a person to a collection of things that needed to be dealt with.

Mike's brother broke the silence and asked me if I wanted to know how he did it. I said yes but I already knew. I hated that I knew him so well that I knew how his depression would overcome him. I also hated that he had to be found that way.

'They don't need to do an autopsy because the cause of death is, well, yeah ...'

'I'm sorry.' If he didn't find him, I knew it would have been me. I didn't know which I would have preferred.

We sat in even more silence, trying not to fall apart in front of each other.

'Did you want to take something of his to remember him by?' I wanted it all. I wanted his books, his travel souvenirs, his ugly acid-wash overalls that he never fully buckled, his jewellery, his plants, his reading glasses. In the end, I settled for one of his leather jackets that had moulded to his body shape, the pits sweat-stained and the pockets so tattered his keys always ended up jingling around in the space between the lining and the leather. It was the jacket he wore the most. It was filthy. It stunk of him.

'Smell is very powerful to the memory,' Mike's dad said when he asked me what I took. Mike's parents were sitting in the neighbour's lounge surrounded by dogs, struggling to sip cups of tea. We were all trying to hold it together for each other. None of us knew what to do.

When I got home, I hung up Mike's jacket to maintain the shape, but I didn't want to air it out. I hid it in a closet with no air flow in the back of the apartment. Sometimes, his brother asks if I am wearing the jacket, but I can't bring myself to. I don't want to dilute the smell. Nowadays, it's faint, but it is there. The stench of life. The stench of better times.

'I was wondering if you had any images of Mike you could send me,' wrote his mother. Slideshows of the dead living their best lives were now commonplace in funerals. The last time I went to the funeral of a friend who had died by suicide, the smiling faces and lively action shots felt like they were only there to comfort people in the room and prevent them from asking why.

'I'll send you everything I have.'

'Would you like to say something at the funeral?'

'I can.' I didn't know if I was capable.

'I was also wondering if you could be a pallbearer.' I pictured the casket drooping to one side due to my height. I was advised not to view his body. It was for the best. Carrying him into a hearse would be the only physical way I could help my brain to understand that he was gone, and not just studying or overseas. The longest we'd been separated was three months when he travelled in India, and I'd still received messages from him every day. My phone was maddeningly quiet.

'I can do that.'

I opened the gallery of my phone and searched all the images of Mike's face. I didn't have many photos. He was the one who documented our lives. All of the images of us lived in deactivated accounts or in locked up technology. I thought about all the times we did stupid shit in dodgy places all over the city; I thought of us sitting in cocktail bars in Manhattan, eating tacos in a tortilla factory in Brooklyn and sharing a lobster on Valentine's Day, just because. He had all those photos. He had the photos of us in wine bars when he flew from the west coast to the east coast to see me for five days because he just happened to be in California visiting family while I was in New York for work. He was the sentimental one and I had nothing to show for it.

I clicked on our text message thread and searched our media. There were hundreds of video messages that he'd sent me – exam prep, selfies of outfits to approve, photos of him flexing because he was 'coming for me', him in changing rooms wanting to know if he should buy items of clothing that looked like items of clothing he already owned, meals he was eating, chickens he had roasted, bread he was baking, dogs he was patting. I sent them all.

I looked at his assigned profile photo and it was a grotesque mashup of our faces with too many teeth, four eyebrows, fat lips and a beard. A friend of ours had overlaid these photos of us after Mike asked if he could have my eggs. I had no intention of ever having children, but Mike said he wanted ours. The plan was to have them in the most unnatural way possible. A petri dish, his sperm, my eggs, the womb of a hospitality friend who wanted to stay in the country and could lie about being in a long-term, committed relationship with Mike, then a baby. In Mike's mind, the child would have the best parts of the both of us. It would be a super-hot, ambitious, whip-smart realist, half-country kid, half third-generation-Cantonese kid who could annihilate you physically and verbally. I said it would probably end up with his chicken legs, my flat face and our neuroses, squared. According to the photo, it would be a disgrace. I promised him my eggs, saying he had to deal with my mood swings in extracting them, but also saved the photo as his profile picture as a permanent warning. In the future Mike wrote for us, we stupidly had kids.

I sent the photo to his mother with the backstory hoping to at least make her laugh. She thanked me for the photo dump, and didn't ask any questions about the endless stream of topless flexing. She knew what was up.

'Hey, I haven't heard from you in ages. What's going on?' My old trainer wasn't much for texting as he was always on the go. I'd forgotten how strong his Irish accent was.

'There's no easy way to say this. You know Mike who was training at your gym?'

'Which classes was he doing?'

'BJJ. Dark-brown hair, shaved head, covered in tatts.'

'Oh yeah, Mike. Great guy. Is he your boy?'

I took a deep breath and scatter-gunned my response. 'Best mate. He passed away. And I'm trying to help his mother find his white quartz necklace. Do you know if it's turned up in lost property?'

'Shit, Jess. I'll look for it. Let us know if we can do anything, if there's a service we can attend. Is it okay if I pass it on to the crew? He had quite a few friends here.'

In our discussions about depression and hanging on, I'd recommended Mike get back into physical activity because training always regulated my mood. He did yoga for a few years after injuring himself snowboarding but lost the love. I suggested a martial art. I told him that it's about learning a discipline and knowing there is always someone better than you. Plus I told him that fighting was like playing violent chess, which immediately piqued his interest. I warned him against striking sports because of his broken wrist, and he settled for BJJ, which I described as a sport where you viciously hug people into submission while wearing pyjamas. Mike was insanely competitive, so he fell in love with it. It was his one focus outside of study.

'Yeah. Thanks. His family are from regional Victoria, but we'll hold a Melbourne memorial. I'll let you know about it, and feel free to invite the gym.'

'I'll let you know about the necklace.'

'Thanks.'

'Jess. I'm really sorry.'

'Me too.' I hung up.

The necklace was gone. After tearing apart the apartment looking for it, Mike's brother checked the last photo he took of Mike and noticed he wasn't wearing the stone. We concluded that he'd lost it.

I couldn't sleep. Part of me was unable to sleep, and the other part of me refused to sleep. There was no logic to it, but I was afraid to forget parts of him by falling asleep and putting days between him being alive and him being dead. I'd lay in bed devastated at how determined he must have been to end his life.

In my loneliest, darkest moment where I couldn't even bring myself to call Mike, I'd want my life to end, but not to necessarily end my own life. I wanted nothingness and unconsciousness, but I didn't have the will to plan.

As I continued to speak to people and break the news of Mike's death, people who had never experienced suicidal ideation would make comments about how it was a selfish act. They didn't understand the isolation of depression, and the lies it tells you. Even though I told Mike every single day that I loved him, in those final moments, he felt alone. His brain told him he was out of options. Suicide isn't a selfish act. Suicide is the final symptom of depression.

I'd think about the last time I saw Mike. I was in the city picking up a passport renewal form from the post office after a meeting. I saw him sitting outside on a bench staring into space. He didn't even notice I was there until I slid next to him and gave him a hug. It was the first time in our friendship that he'd jumped at my touch. In the past we would have talked shit until one of us had to leave, but Mike made an excuse to go to uni and texted me later, apologising for being spaced out. He said he hadn't spoken to anyone all day and felt weird talking to me. It was never a problem before, and I knew he wasn't going to class at all.

'Do you need me to swaddle you in a blanket and hug you until you fall asleep?' I wrote.

'Yes. But I also want to be alone.'

'Let me know if you need me.'

'I will.' We exchanged I love yous and I didn't hear from him until the next day, which was the equivalent of years of silence for us. I made a point of texting him if I hadn't heard from him on his morning dog walk with messages like, 'Blatantly checking in on you and telling you that I love you, dickhead.'

I'd crawl from my bed to the couch to stay awake and log in to my streaming services. I shared my accounts with Mike. There were all these unfinished series waiting for him, now with even more seasons to go. There were shows we were watching together, which have remained untouched since he died. This was the end of their stories.

It occurred to me that when Mike's mother asked me to say something at his funeral, she meant I'd be giving a eulogy. All the stories I had were inappropriate or would make us sound like we were a couple. People were already treating me like I was a grieving widow, and I didn't want any more of that.

I couldn't say that I felt sorry for everyone who wasn't us because our friendship made us impervious to everything. I couldn't say that all our partners had to accept the fact that we came as a joint package. I couldn't say that we nursed each other out of addictions. I couldn't say that we argued like siblings and would only hold ceasefires to laugh at other peoples' misfortunes. I couldn't say that I can't enjoy the rain without him. I couldn't say that I can't have a single thought without telling him about it. I couldn't say that I was completely lost without him. Most of all, I couldn't say that I understood why he chose to leave.

You're not supposed to understand. You're supposed to be angry that they didn't stay.

Eventually, I wrote some word vomit that was acceptable to deliver to a room of grieving people. The venue requested my words in advance so they could print it out in excessive, size twenty-two font and slip it into a plastic sleeve on the lectern so I could read it without stumbling.

I flew to Mildura in one of those tiny tin cans that you can feel every single bump in, and I remembered all the photographs Mike had sent me from the plane every time he went home. Now, I was sitting among it. Oversized white t-shirts, worn-out thongs, faded board shorts and mullets. From our first meeting, I never would have picked that he came from a town known for citrus and sunburn.

The service was huge. Mike's family saved me a seat towards the front, and every time I looked around, it felt like a hundred more people turned up. By the time the funeral began, there were people standing, filling up all the room behind the pews, into the foyer and out to the car park.

Mike's father told the story of Mike's birth, his energy as a child, his sacrifice as a young adult, and illustrated how he was a cheeky little shit with a story about a time he stuck inappropriate signs made of post-its on his unsuspecting colleagues. His lecturer recorded a tribute about Mike's brilliance as a student and wholeness as a human. One of Mike's close friends told the story of how they ripped through Japan on the scrapings of their savings. When it came time for me to speak, I choked through my words. I stared into a room of hundreds of distorted faces holding in breaths, red in the eyes, and it knocked the composure out of me. I struggled through telling everyone how Mike taught me to love, having to suck down all the air around me after every third word. My face was hot and full of tears. It was the first time I cried after Mike had died. I was thankful for the double-spaced, size twenty-two font so I could reach the end of his story.

I held my breath as we carried Mike's casket into the hearse. I knew the weight of Mike's body from piggybacking him through the streets, from when he jumped on me for hugs, from him leaning on me for support after a big night. Now, I knew what his dead weight felt like.

Watching the car drive away with his body made my chest physically hurt, like someone reached in, wrung out my lungs and crushed my heart inside their fist. I turned around to look for a familiar face, but was surrounded by ones I didn't know, telling me they were sorry for my loss, and that Mike loved me very much. The only faces I knew from his past were blood or ex-girlfriends. These were the faces that grew up with him.

I found Mike's father and he gave me a hug. 'It was true love I heard come out of you, every quiver, every cry,' he said. Even though I tried not to, I made myself sound like a mourning widow. It didn't matter what I said, having a public meltdown cemented my place.

There was a small lunch provided in the back of the venue and the room stank of tomato sauce. The vinegar in the air burned my nose hairs. I learned that party pies, sausage rolls and finger sandwiches filled with pickle relish were customary Australian funeral foods.

I went into town with a group of Mike's city friends before the wake at the family home. We went to the only place that was open, a pub, and ate hot chips. I chugged glasses of water because I realised I hadn't eaten in days and was dehydrated from crying. I went out the front to get some air and I was stopped by a tall guy around my age in a beanie with long, brown hair. He was inconsolable and told me how much Mike meant to him. They were primary-school friends, and he said Mike was the first person who really saw him. He followed us from the funeral home just to tell me that and disappeared around the corner after he'd blurted it out.

When we got to the family home, I matched up areas of the house to photos Mike had sent me. There was the pool he used to splash about in, collecting sun damage and justifying his lack of showers. There was the couch in the sunken lounge room where he'd be assaulted by his parents' dogs. Sosu nibbled at my shoelaces. Mike's parents had decided to take her in. There was the pergola in the front yard where he'd ceremoniously drink red wine and smoke cigarettes with his mother.

His dad took me to the backyard where he fed the budgies. I

watched him robotically take a bag of seeds, tossing them in the air, yelling, 'Guinea, guinea, guinea,' before a rush of guinea hens pecked at the ground and dispersed. His face was pained, and I could see that he found it pointless keeping all these birds alive when a major part of his family had disappeared forever.

I went back to the hotel before the sun went down, to his family's disappointment. I caught the end of *Leaving Neverland* then passed out on the lumpy hotel bed. I woke up in the same position I'd fallen asleep in, exhausted, and packed my stuff to check out and board a flight, knowing I had to do this all over again in the city with his 'grown-up' friends.

Mike's Japan friend and I begrudgingly resorted to creating a Facebook event for his Melbourne memorial. It was crude but necessary, because everyone changed their numbers so regularly and I had no other way to contact Mike's exes. I titled it *The Life and Opinions of Mike Barker, Gentleman*, because we wanted a less formal, celebratory tone to the day, but no one picked up on the reference.

It created an unfortunate amount of gossip among the Melbourne hospitality network. One particular idiot copped a 'You fucking what, now?' from me when he publicly announced the event to his group of friends on the street like he'd just fucked his first crush. The spineless piece of shit did not show up to the memorial.

The day descended into debauchery. After a series of speeches that ranged from abstract to heartfelt, that at times felt like it was a Mike-themed open mic night, people drank to commemorate him to the point where they fell off their stools. The martial arts crew came to honour Mike's memory, stayed sober, lined up to offer their condolences to Mike's family and said they were going to frame his gi in the studio. It was the most respectful response I'd seen from anyone in his circle.

Mike's mother smirked at me from across the room when she realised I was cornered by a procession of his exes wanting to tell me how much love they had for him. When I was finally relieved of duty, she said, 'I knew he shared it around quite a bit.' I told her it felt like I was a roadie being accosted by a brigade of groupies, all hoping I could sneak them into the greenroom while bumping out the concert.

I met up with Mike's brother and neighbour a week after. He gave us tubes of Mike's ashes. Mike's neighbour scattered her portion under a huge tree, and I thought about how cremated remains are mostly calcium phosphate that can burn the soil if not distributed properly. I imagined this epic tree shrivelling up and dying, and how Mike would laugh at the kind intention resulting in disaster. But in reality there weren't enough of his remains to cause any change to the soil. I hoped a dog wouldn't sniff him out and piss on him.

When I got home, I held Mike's ashes and stared at them, wondering which parts of him I'd received. I wondered if it was the cyst on his forearm that he liked to play with when he was bored, or his fingers that didn't work, or his front tooth that was actually a veneer, or his chest that he inflated when he wanted to command attention. I wondered if it was the mandala he'd tattooed on his skull, which I gave him crap for because my understanding of mandalas was that they symbolised impermanence. But now, the mandala was ash and could be brushed away, swept up and washed down a stream, as intended. Mike always played the long game. 'You've won this round,' I said to Mike, and put him in the fruit bowl so he'd be the first thing I saw every morning.

This was the end of our story.

13

Everything hurt.

I was physically and mentally crushed.

I'd just flown back to Melbourne in economy through many redirected and delayed flights from San Francisco, where I'd watched an aunt who cared for me deeply, but who hardly knew me, die.

The year had been filled with deaths. Deaths from failed systems, from domestic violence, from cancer and it wasn't even July.

The wine bar had been open for over two years, but I could only leave it for a week because no one else could handle the kitchen on busy nights and I was stretching the budget by overstaffing. A few days before I left, my dad called me and said his sister, his last living relative from his immediate family, was dying. She was diagnosed with late-stage ovarian cancer again and couldn't bear to go through treatment when the chances of survival were so slim. She had assessed her entire life up until this point and was satisfied with her experiences, her close relationships, and her legacy. Her body gave her an ultimatum and she decided that she was ready to go.

'Your cousin said to come sooner rather than later. She is very bad. Not good. Very not good. I go next week. If you want to go, you go now.' My dad rarely called me because all his communication was monitored by my mother. I received one Whatsapp message from him a year that was either on New Year's or my birthday. He was never allowed to see me on his own, so I just didn't see him. We decided it was easier to get through life disconnected than punctuated by the wrath of my mother. Rarer still was him speaking to me in English. He wanted to be sure I understood the severity of the situation. Even travelling was something he never did because of his immigrant guilt. He was breaking all the rules. This was no time to fuck around.

'How long are you going for?'

'I go one week, then your mother come a week later. Two week, maybe three.' It was a blessing that I could only afford a week.

Before the Handover, my family had relocated to either San Francisco or Melbourne, and we were too poor to visit each other. I didn't meet my aunt until I was a teenager, which meant my dad hadn't see his sisters for at least thirteen years. Every year before that, without fail, my aunt would send me a card and a super trendy American gift for my birthday. My family didn't believe in gifts or buying off the shelf (so expensive), so in my mind, she was rich and regal. She also openly embraced American culture, which my parents refused to do with Australia, so she represented an open-hearted kind of freedom that I always craved. When we finally did meet, she was warm, nurturing and liberal. She was everything I was lacking in my life. I didn't want her to leave. But now, she was ready to die.

I heard the melancholy in my dad's voice. He'd spent the last few years watching all his siblings die, and all of them were before their time. He grieved silently and invisibly behind closed doors. There was no room for empathy in the family home.

'I'll book a ticket now. Can you let everyone know I'm coming over?'

'Okay, bye-bye.' He ended the conversation abruptly and with a high note, because his only English language send-off was a cheery one.

I sat my staff down, told them what was happening and asked them to send me daily reports and concerns because I would bring my laptop with me. It was only a week.

I set them up for success by overstaffing, preparing everything in advance, ordering goods a few days early and not changing the food or drink menu for a week. All they needed to do was show up on time and do the bare minimum.

I didn't allow my body to adjust to San Franciscan time. I was still running according to the Melbourne clock to make sure I could handle any concerns sent to me at the end of the night.

By the second day, I'd been told that someone was so over the limit that they threw up all over their table, and that another staff member kept turning up to work without showering after partying all night.

Minutes after receiving these emails, I watched a nurse lay my aunt down on the couch – she lived with my cousins – and show my cousins how to drain the fluid that was collecting in her abdomen to relieve her pain. I'd watch my aunt force her eyes closed, praying for comfort. My cousins would practise inserting tubes into her, as well as the proper way to remove things from her body, sterilise and dispose of them.

'This might have to be done several times a day,' the nurse told my cousins.

I looked at the draft of my email responding to vomit and lack of personal hygiene and wondered how I'd ended up in charge of children older than me. I hit send.

My cousins looked heartbroken. My uncle couldn't bear to watch what was happening to his wife and he hid in the kitchen, preparing school lunches for my cousins' teenage children.

This was the first time in my life I had met my cousins or spent any real time with my father as an adult. My cousins saw each other daily. Their kids were the same age, and they all went to the same school. They carpooled and would always do after-school snacks together. The kids would go off to do their homework and they'd eat dinner together around the kitchen table. I had never seen this before. I'd also never seen my dad happier in his entire life.

'You're all so wholesome,' I said to my cousin.

'Wholesome? This is normal.'

'Yeah, all my friends are like this too. Sometimes they join us,' said my cousin's daughter. I stood there with my mouth open in disbelief, like an idiot.

I called my sister and reported my findings. We had started speaking regularly after she left the family home. It was safe for us to talk. Finally.

'Oh my god, Jess, that *is* normal. We were so neglected and abused. Do our cousins think you're mental?'

'I think they feel sorry for us. And Dad. They especially feel sorry for Dad.'

'How is Dad?'

'Happy and sad, in both extremes, at the same time. I'm going to take him out for lunch tomorrow and he is super excited.'

'Of course he is. It's like he's been broken out of jail.'

I took my dad to one of the city's classic restaurants – the kind of restaurant a local would describe as 'quintessential'. He kept asking me for permission to order things, and I kept having to tell him he was allowed to order whatever he wanted because my mother wasn't here to say no. I could see his brain short-circuiting. When he finally made his decision, we ordered cocktails, anchovies, a woodfire roast chicken, chips and a bottle of Chardonnay from the Jura.

This was the first time we'd hung out since I left home and he was still afraid to make a connection with me, even though it was quite possibly the drunkest he had ever been in his life. His face was flushed, and he grinned the entire ride on the BART back to my cousin's house.

I watched my dad slumped in his seat with a smile and I knew this was the story I'd tell at his funeral. It took over a decade, a dying relative, an eighteen-hour time difference and the only time my parents had been physically separated from one another for us to finally have lunch, and he still couldn't have a real conversation with me. This was it. There would be no other chance.

When we busted through the front door and my dad used me to steady himself so he could remove his shoes, my aunt laughed at the state of him then held my hand while asking me how my day was before she went to bed. She was in pain the entire time I was there, but my cousins said our visit lifted her spirits.

She died shortly after my dad came back to Melbourne. I found out via a text message from my cousin as I was setting the kitchen up for service. I'd have to push it to the back of my mind because when people go out for a drink, they're looking for a shoulder and an ear, not the other way around.

I listened to other people's problems all night. I nodded along to the rant about unjust, rising prices of cigarettes from a lifelong smoker whose father and grandfather had both died of lung cancer. 'It's my choice, dammit!' I poured glass after glass for a man who confessed to the whole bar that he proudly touted his Trumpist ideas in online newspaper comment sections, and that renewable energy was a conspiracy theory against the rich. 'Wake me up when this is all over.' I furrowed my brow at the appropriate times when a group of single women lamented over the ineligible bachelors at a singles event they just attended. 'At least iron your shirt!' I poured shots for a local resident whose favourite race horse would have to be retired after a series of underwhelming performances. 'He made me some great money over the years.' I feigned interest at a camera roll of dirt when a developer showed me the site where they'd just broken ground. 'Look at this sexy soil.' I made myself scarce when a couple on the last legs of their relationship started arguing over dinner. 'I *asked* you if you wanted any bread. I would have *ordered* extra bread because now you're just eating *my* bread.' I played along with a rescue mission for someone on a Tinder date. 'If I order a glass of sauvignon blanc, get me out of this as fast as you can.'

And then a woman came in. She was a columnist who had recently lost her column in a restructure. A woman who, for some reason, had once thought I was relevant. A woman who made a living off reporting gossip, and who had herself been made irrelevant by Twitter, Instagram and camera phones. 'I've been told that I *must* have that fennel salami,' she said while seating herself at a four-top, even though she was a single diner.

'Are you just stopping in for a snack or would you like to see the menu?' I had no idea why she'd come in purely to eat a cured meat that I'd bought in from a distributor. She could eat it anywhere. There were venues known for making their own salumi – we were not one of them.

'Oh, just bring me a few things. I have half an hour.'

'Wine?'

'Something white. Whatever you reckon.'

'Still or sparkling water?'

'Sparkling.' I cleared off the other covers, poured her a cheap, crowd-pleasing number that drank well above its price along with her water and walked into the kitchen to put together her food. The crew member I was working with stuck his face over the pass and rolled his eyes at me over her taking up a four-top. 'I know,' I mouthed.

I walked over a series of snacks, making the executive decision to give her half-serves so she could sample an array. Without even looking up at me as I explained what I had given her, she started picking at the plates and chewing with her mouth open. She raised her index finger and double tapped on the rim of her empty wine glass.

'A top-up?' I asked.

She only nodded in response.

When I came back with the bottle and a new wine glass, she grabbed my wrist with her greasy salami hand and said, 'You know, I didn't know what you were doing these days until your business partner told me. I bumped into him when I had a coffee today.' The only reason I'd agreed to open this wine bar was because my business partner was a silent one. Wine, professional service and night-time dining weren't his space. He was a divisive figure in the industry, and it seemed that he couldn't keep his mouth shut. I stared intensely at the fennel seed caught in the ridge between her incisor and her canine. 'Because you really peaked when you did the social media and hosting for that restaurant,' she went on. I realised the only reason she chewed with her mouth open was that her lips were so full of filler she couldn't close them.

I looked her directly in the eye and then at her hand. She immediately let go of my wrist.

'Everyone's entitled to their opinion,' I said, with a disingenuous smile.

I walked behind the bar to add another glass to her bill, and my colleague whispered in my ear, 'Did she just say what I thought she just said?'

'Yep.'

'Does she know what irony is?' He came from a series of large-profile restaurants so he knew media faces the same way he knew wine labels.

'Clearly not.'

She demolished everything in front of her, leaving a fingerpainting of olive oil on the natural stone table.

'Do you need to go? Would you like the bill?' I asked.

'Your business partner said he would shout me a meal. I can show you his text message.'

'No need. I'll sort it out.' Another freebie whore.

The bar cleared out suddenly, which was normal for a school night. We took advantage of the break in service and I cleaned down the kitchen while my crew member restocked.

'Eleven for a Monday, not bad,' I said, 'I'm gonna call it. Wanna sign off and I can do the till?'

'Yeah, thanks.' I poured him a knock-off, texted my cousin to ask how she was doing, and cashed out. No response.

'Are you not having a drink?'

'I'm not feeling it.'

'Over it?'

'Over it.' We both fell into hospitality because it came easy to us. We were good at it, but we had less stable, creative interests that always managed to crawl to the front of our minds. He was hiding out working with me while he decided between perusing his passion or being set up for life in another large, meaningless, wine job. Up until this point, we had both chosen security. I kept making space to put my degree to use, but at every junction, I was presented with an offer that could buy me a comfortable financial position for at least a few years.

'I think I'm gonna sell,' I said.

'You should. One of us at least should get out of this industry.'

'I'm sick of it.'

'What, specifically?'

'Everything hurting.'

I wasn't even thirty yet, but I had to line my shoes with two sets of inner soles just so I could walk without wincing. Every single finger was cracked and bleeding from being constantly wet, dipped in chemicals, running dishwashers and polishing glassware. My back hurt from lugging my office equipment to and from home every day because I couldn't afford an office space. My calves screamed from constantly standing on my toes to reach for items behind the bar and in the kitchen. My neck was locked from tension, heavy lifting and working in spaces built for taller people, and I hadn't been able to turn my head to the right in months. My ears hadn't stopped ringing from years spent standing under gigantic speakers while people shouted their names at me. My stomach churned constantly because for six days a week, all I could eat were offcuts of bread dipped in anything softer than bread. My heart ached over all the people I'd lost whom I had no time to mourn. My brain was tired from having to deal with racists or sleazebags, or racist sleazebags, or entitled customers asking me if they could speak to the owner while pointing at a staff member, drunks who would follow me home at night, people who treated me like a thing and not a person. My throat was sore from forcing a higher, softer register than my natural speaking voice so I could sound as white and trustworthy as possible, because people still couldn't get their heads around a young, Asian vagina-owner giving wine recommendations or having industry experience. My face was numb from my fake-arse, shit-eating smile.

I did the logical thing and offered my silent partner my share of the business. He accepted without hesitation.

'So, you're leaving me.'

'I guess so.'

'Why?'

'I use contraception for a reason. I don't want a baby. That's what owning a venue and having staff is: a big, shit-throwing, tantrum-having, disobedient baby.' The truth was it was worse. I had a lot of hospo friends who had children and they said kids were nothing compared to running a venue. I took their word for it.

'That is a very fair reason.' He shook my hand and that was that.

I broke the news to my staff and assured them they would still have jobs if they wished to stay on. Aside from the crew member who closed with me the other evening, who had been quietly working on his folio, the staff were not happy. I was abandoning them. A month was too soon. What about their dreams?

See, a big baby.

'I never intended to have this forever. I have nothing else to give,' I said.

'What if he wants to change everything?'

'He's allowed to change things. It will be entirely his business. I'm sure if any of you approached him with the cash to buy my share of the business, he would be smart enough to consider it.'

'Don't you care?'

'It's not mine to care about anymore.' It took all my willpower not to tell them that I had no sentimental feelings towards a bar and an industry that had abused, stalked, harassed, sexually assaulted, intimidated, belittled, gaslit, bullied, discarded and overworked me. I was going to receive my payout. There was nothing left for me to care about anymore. It's a drinks list and a food menu, not a treaty for world peace.

'What about your legacy?'

'Legacy is an illusion for people who are in denial about their own insignificance.' I couldn't wait to be insignificant. To disappear.

I compiled handover documents, spreadsheets of passwords, ordering instructions, names of reps and directions on how to fix everything that tended to break for no reason during the busiest times. I knew no one would read them, but I did not want anyone to call me after I clocked out for the final time. It was the right thing to do. Covering my arse was always the right thing to do.

In my final week, I told the regulars that I was leaving. I did not expect to have so many people who emotionally connected me to their drinking habits. For some of them, I made their everyday drinking acceptable. My compulsion to keep everyone topped up with water meant that they rarely woke up with a hangover. I would sometimes make dishes that weren't on the menu for an engineer with a fly-in-fly-out job, which is the reason he would drink through the by-the-glass list on his weeks back in Melbourne. The local hospitality cohort heard whispers of me leaving, and when I confirmed it, they reminisced over Tuesday nights (my Friday) when I would deep-fry bags' worth of chips and make gravy from the fat trimmed from prosciutto and dregs of spirit samples. Then I'd lay it out on the bar so everyone could help themselves while they purchased high-end bottles to smash after service. A local couple confessed that they would do drive-bys and only come in if I was working. Musicians from the string section of Opera Australia thanked me for always finding a space for their equipment during their post-rehearsal drink. A lawyer thanked me for always allowing him to buy a full bottle, extract half of it through a Coravin and let him finish it on his next visit. A couple of locals asked me to write down the style of wine I always sold them to take home to their partners when they dropped in for a cheeky beer. A mortician who loved to let loose in front of me insisted we catch up once I left since it would no longer be unprofessional to drink with her. Every single person asked me if I was going to open another venue.

I knew a lot of things about the regulars. I knew their likes and dislikes, when they were going through break-ups, the names of their pets, how they met their partners, where they went on holiday, how many children they had, what they were going to have for dinner that night, embarrassing stories, but they knew nothing about me. They believed my smile. They thought my life's dream was to be Sam Malone.

'If I'm still serving the same alcoholics in the same neighbourhood bar when I reach the age of retirement, I know I have failed,' said another bar owner when I stopped by his venue to tell him I was leaving the hood. 'Congratulations.' My first congratulations. 'I'm not worried about you. You will land on your feet. What's next?'

'I've already been commissioned to write a bunch of commercial content. My god, it's good money.' The best thing about writing commercial content was the absence of a byline. I really could disappear for a while.

'Freelance for a bit?'

'Yeah, I can afford to. The first thing I am going to do is turn my phone off and sleep for a week.'

'Only a week?' I was speaking to a seasoned pro. He'd opened and sold numerous venues all over the city, and even had his fingers in overseas projects.

'Deadlines.'

He gave me a bear hug and said, 'Trust me. You'll sleep for more than a week.'

I slowly realised the only people who were genuinely happy for me were other hands-on small business owners. We communicated in shorthand because there was no need to go through the struggles of the day, discuss the headache of maintaining and finding staff, or to justify any of the ruthless and pragmatic decisions we made in order to keep the wheels turning. We were all Mean Mummy.

When I saw each of their faces drop for a millisecond, despite their genuine happiness for me, I knew how privileged I was. I did not have a family at home to support. I was not finishing the degree I abandoned in my teens and paying mature-age tertiary study fees. I was not running a prestigious generational family business that had the weight of industry expectation on its shoulders. I was not paying spousal maintenance. I had no child support fees. I didn't own a designer dog that required multiple operations just so it could breathe. I didn't even have a car I had to make payments on. My life was spartan.

I could walk away from what had always proven to be stable. I had the luxury of risk. I always thought I was disadvantaged because I didn't have a single, specialised focus. Everyone else was amazing at their *thing*. They knew everything about their *thing* whereas I knew a little bit about a lot. It made me a chameleon and gave me the confidence to leave. I wasn't trapped in the chef box, the wine box, the bartender box, the manager box, the host box, or the waiter box. I wouldn't be leaving this role only to do the same role somewhere else. I didn't have a mental block when trying something new. I had choices.

I had to explain to my non-hospo friends that I had nothing to justify. I had nothing to prove. Hospitality wasn't my personality. It wasn't my life. But their understanding of the industry was all cooking shows, Marco Pierre White, Anthony Bourdain, Gordon

Ramsay and their feeling of being a diner, receiving the bullshit and the performance without knowing it's just bullshit and a performance. In their heads, the industry was a safe space. It was a cruisy, glamourous, drama-free, money-making cash cow. These were the people who liked to take the day off on their birthdays, and I had to explain to them that I had worked every public holiday since I was legally allowed to work. For me, a win was coincidentally being rostered off on Valentine's Day so I could stay home and sleep. I reminded them that they stopped inviting me to everything years ago because I was always working, and calling in sick was not an option. I also told them that if their dream was to quit their job and open a cafe, they should find a new dream because it would be more efficient to withdraw their life savings in cash, put it in a barrel and light it on fire.

A lot of them asked what I would do next, assuming the only skill I had accumulated over the years was the ability to carry multiple plates at once. The truth is, growing up in the industry forces you to teach semiotics, think laterally, make quick decisions, perform first aid, learn accounting, pick up marketing skills, throw massive events, network, manage people, liaise with councils, copywrite, be your own tech support, act and serve. In my own experience from hiring people, I knew that the most qualified person didn't always get the job. There is a saying among managers that you can teach anyone how to carry a plate, but you can't teach someone how to not be a cunt.

My plan was simple: don't be a cunt.

I texted the small producers I dealt with directly and let them know who would oversee ordering when I left. One of them responded with, 'Is this a good thing or a bad thing?'

'A good thing. Why?'

'You strike me as the kind of person who wants to be the best at everything,' he wrote.

'I have nothing else I want to do or get out of this industry.'

'What do you mean?' He was young, ambitious and hell-bent on winning awards and breaking into the international market.

'Let me ask you a question. When you see a local Chinese restaurant close, what do you think has happened?'

'They've gone broke.'

'Sometimes, yes. But for those who have been there for many years, it has served its purpose.'

'I don't get it.'

'A lot of Chinese restaurants started because it was the only way for immigrant families to make money. Their degrees weren't recognised, and a widely accepted product of any immigrant family is their food. This restaurant generates money to house, feed and educate the family. A success story is when a restaurant closes because the parents want to retire and their kids can't take over the business because they have their own careers. It's a good thing when the kids are too useless to know how to use a wok.'

'Right.'

'This venue and my time in the industry have served their purpose.'

I felt like I was breaking up with someone I'd been in a relationship with for far too long. In the beginning, it was fun. I was obsessed with learning everything I could about it and I was happy to walk into work every day. In the middle, I saw it for who it was. I was going through the motions. I was living alongside it. I was tolerating the things about it that annoyed me, didn't talk about the terrible things that were happening in case someone told me I deserved better, and I focused on the good shit. I took a break and explored my options, but I found myself back in hospo because it was safe and familiar. In the end, I recognised how co-dependent and toxic it was. Somehow, I grew up and changed, but the industry, as much as I put into it, was the same.

Even though the relationship soured, I got a lot out of it. It helped me find my chosen family. It taught me how to connect with people and how to tell a great story. It let me peek into different tiers of society, taught me to trust, taught me to be a more cynical person, taught me to be a tolerant person. It taught me to be adaptable and know which battles were worth fighting, and it forced me to realise what kind of a person I didn't want to be.

Hospitality gave me a crash course in how to be a functional human. It allowed me to feel normal among all the people with broken brains who were also trying to be less broken. We all ran towards the noise to make the noise in our lives feel like the quiet.

When I closed the doors to my bar for the last time and handed over the keys, I did not feel sadness. I didn't need it anymore.

For the last time, I walked home by myself in the early hours of the morning, feeling like I was being baptised by the street lamps. For the first time, I let myself stop. When I got into bed, I turned off my phone and allowed myself the luxury of unmeasured sleep. As I lost consciousness, I didn't delude myself by thinking I'd wake up and be a productive member of society, but I knew I was finally ready to participate in it.

Epilogue

It's Friday night and we have driven half an hour to the suburbs of Melbourne to eat at a non-descript Cantonese restaurant in a run-down shopping strip, a restaurant that has not been written about in any broadsheet or lifestyle magazine. The owners bought it a year ago from the last family who owned the place because they were regulars and still wanted somewhere to hang out. One of the new owners also used to be a chef in Hong Kong.

We are here because I heard they make the best Pipa duck going around. This is a huge deal because usually when I eat duck in Melbourne, I'm disappointed. I can't help but compare it to Hong Kong barbecue shops. They are the ultimate.

I'm with an old hospo friend who now owns five of the most loved and hyped inner-city venues; a professional baker; and a second-generation Vietnamese friend whose family ran one of the longest-established restaurants on Victoria Street. He migrated back to Vietnam a few years ago but he's back for a holiday. Despite my making money as a freelance food journo, these people still associate with me. They joke that I'm 'hospo-retired' and out of touch after four years off the floor. Our friendships range from years to over a decade. As we get out of the car, we walk past five older Chinese men in wifebeaters smoking cigarettes, clutching young bottles of Grange, giving each other shit about how much money each of them lost on the horses today.

'We're in the right place,' says my friend visiting from Vietnam. He too, has a bottle of Grange, only his bottle has been properly cellared and is ready to drink because it's older than me. He's in on the joke, but he also has taste. As soon as we're seated, one of the waiters whisks the wine away, breaks the cork, rescues it and empties the bottle into the shittiest wine glasses I have ever seen. There is sediment in every glass.

The restaurant looks as run down inside as it does outside. The specials are all written in traditional script on the walls, the female toilet doubles as a supply closet and the fish tanks have tens of thousands of dollars worth of seafood swimming around in them. The sound system is pumping out cringy Cantonese covers of American nineties pop songs. There is a help-yourself fridge next to the register filled with cans of Coke and Yakult. Everyone is drunk, shouting and eating crab. Some tables have even BYO-ed multiple bottles of baiju.

'I think I used to come here a decade ago. It wasn't very memorable.'

'There are new owners,' I say. 'I've pre-ordered the winter

melon soup and Pipa duck. How do you feel about crab?'

'I want all of it,' says my friend visiting from Vietnam.

'Happy for you to order,' says Baker.

'My favourite atmosphere is no atmosphere,' says Restaurateur, taking it all in, deeply aware that all his restaurants have great atmosphere and are heavily designed.

'I don't like to pay for atmosphere,' I say to him, and he laughs.

One of the owners comes around with a whole cooked winter melon filled with a viscous, delicate, seafood-studded soup, and he starts ladling out its contents while scraping the sides of the fibrous vegetable into small bowls.

'That's the way, that's the way,' says Vietnamese Friend, filming the whole process on his phone. We each break out our phones to capture the spectacle of the soup, setting aside our social graces to document a bit of Cantonese tradition hidden in the outer suburbs.

'Did you want to order anything else?' says the owner to me in Cantonese. 'You've also got the duck. Do you want crab?' What an upsell.

'Yes please. On sticky rice and lotus leaf.'

'What type of crab?'

'Snow.' I also order a tofu dish that comes with preserved Chinese olive and minced pork that I know no one on the table has eaten before, and a literal bucket of rice.

When the whole splayed and lacquered duck comes out,

everyone's eyes widen. The sweet-savoury fragrance wafts around the table and we can see the fat has been completely rendered from the skin so it shatters like glass. We each pick up a piece of breast meat out of politeness and bite into its flesh.

'I can't believe it is this tender and flavoursome. Nice work, Jess.'

'I didn't cook it!'

Between the four of us, it takes less than fifteen minutes for the duck to disappear, with only the neck and butt left – arguably, the best parts. We spend the next fifteen minutes insisting that the other person on the table enjoy those pieces, using excuses like, 'You're visiting,' or 'You never get to eat out on a Friday night,' or 'You organised it,' or 'I'm saving my stomach for the rest of the food,' until the snow crab is dropped on the table. The duck plate has to be cleared, so the waiter just scrapes the pieces into the closest bowl.

I love this. This is exactly the experience I am chasing.

I've done fine dining to death. I've had access to the most inaccessible experiences, met industry legends who I used to idolise, side-stepped lotteries for exclusive meals, but this is how I like to dine. I don't need the smoke and mirrors. In fact, I don't want them. I don't need flashy service in architectural rooms, a view, or carefully curated playlists. I don't need perfectly temperature-controlled spaces, open kitchens or toilets with designer soaps. I don't need a unicorn-studded wine list or house cocktails made from distillates that can't be categorised. I don't need a reinvention, reinterpretation, refining or deconstruction of a dish that is perfect enough as it is. I don't need food trends, caviar, blown-out livers or truffles from Alba. I don't need plates made by the chef on their day off, bespoke cutlery or a neon sign. I don't want an elevator pitch or a brand identity; I just want some really fucking good food.

Thirty years later, I am still sitting next to the fish tank around a lazy Susan, getting sassed by waiters in my first language, having my bowl filled with herbal soups, roasted birds, tofu and seafood. Only now, I'm stable, content and safe. I'm with the family I've chosen – the ones who have brought me back home.

Acknowledgements

Almost all of this book takes place in Melbourne, the land of the Wurundjeri Woi Wurring people of the Kulin Nation. I pay my respects to their Elders past, present and emerging. I also acknowledge that the people of this land maintain and share knowledge through an oral tradition that has been practised for generations.

Thanks to my agent, Brendan Fredericks, for being my biggest cheerleader. Without you, I'd still be typing angrily into the void. I'd also like to thank Martin Hughes for being my sounding board, guinea pig and voice of reason during the writing process. I still miss our fortnightly exchanges. Ruby Ashby-Orr, you've been the most empathetic and encouraging editor. I am so lucky to have you in my corner and I'm eternally grateful that you took a chance on me.

Graham McKenzie, thank you for everything. The pep talks, the extra classes, the books, the emails, the gossip, and for playing your part in the Queer Kid Befriending the Misunderstood English Teacher trope. I owe you a brandy.

Cin, thank you for reminding me that I'm not crazy and for all those other things that sisters do.

To my friends, thank you for being my family.

Mike, thank you for finding me when you did. I miss you every second of the day.

And finally, Cameron, thanks for putting up with me. I know I'm hard work.